D0085400

INNOVATIONS IN
DEQUITY
FINANCING

INNOVATIONS IN DEQUITY FINANCING

Andrew H. Chen

AND

John W. Kensinger

Quorum Books

NEW YORK • WESTPORT, CONNECTICUT • LONDON

Library of Congress Cataloging-in-Publication Data

Chen, Andrew H.
    Innovations in dequity financing / Andrew H. Chen and John W.
Kensinger.
        p.   cm.
    Includes bibliographical references and index.
    ISBN 0-89930-478-8 (alk. paper)
    1. Corporate debt. 2. Corporations—Finance. 3. Employee
ownership.   I. Kensinger, John W.   II. Title.
HG4028.D3C46   1991
658.15′26—dc20   91-7811

British Library Cataloguing in Publication Data is available.

Library of Congress Catalog Card Number: 91-7811
ISBN: 0-89930-478-8

First published in 1991

Quorum Books, One Madison Avenue, New York, NY   10010
An imprint of Greenwood Publishing Group, Inc.

Printed in the United States of America

∞™

The paper used in this book complies with the
Permanent Paper Standard issued by the National
Information Standards Organization (Z39.48-1984).

10 9 8 7 6 5 4 3 2 1

To Elaine and Betsy

Contents

Exhibits

Preface

This book probes for common threads in the many financial innovations that blended the characteristics of debt and equity. Dequity represents changes that are not just "paper shuffles" or neutral mutations in corporate financial structure. We see the financial trappings as symptoms of far deeper changes. First, much of the debt used in the 1980s has been involved with changes in the structure of ownership and, in particular, an upsurge in the amount of equity owned by employees, albeit purchased with borrowed money. This has been a revolutionary change that will be remembered long after the debt is retired and forgotten and arguably represents the beginning of a remarkable democratization of economic affairs.

A significant increase in aggregate corporate debt in the eighties has arisen from transactions that have radically altered the structure of corporate governance. The control over corporate resources, especially the reinvestment of future cash flows of a corporation, has largely transferred from managers to the lenders. This represents another revolutionary change in the mechanism that controls our economic resources. Once passive institutional investors are becoming activist, and corporate managers are becoming their vassals. Institutional stockholders, who now own about 45 percent of all corporate stock, have become the backbone of a new market for corporate control. Once ready to sell their stock to the highest bidder at a moment's notice, these institutions are now becoming more activist in precipitating changes in the companies that they own. Institutional lenders in leveraged arrangements, too, are becoming more actively involved in the affairs of their debtors.

An additional consequence underlying the financial innovations we examine here is a shift away from owning assets indirectly through corporate stock toward direct ownership of productive assets by investors. While employees are increasingly becoming stockholders and eventually taking their companies private, the companies that remain publicly traded are becoming increasingly hollow and investors are taking title to the buildings, equipment, and natural resources. This is the last thread in the tapestry of change we describe here. We see a trend toward increased specialization of roles, with companies owned and controlled by the people who do the work, while the tools they use are owned by their pension funds, insurance companies, and endowment funds. The new financial hybrids are, in large part, no more than a means to accomplish this transformation.

This book brings together material from several articles we have published in the past five years plus additional material that has not yet been published elsewhere. Chapter 2 is adapted from an article by John Kensinger and John Martin, "The Decline of Public Equity: The Return to Private Enterprise?" published in the November–December 1989 issue of *Business Horizons*.[1] Chapter 3 was originally published by the authors as "Innovations in Corporate Financing: Tax-deductible Equity," in the Winter 1985 issue of *Financial Management*. Chapter 4 is an updated version of "Puttable Stock: A New Innovation in Equity Financing," published in the Spring issue of *Financial Management*. Chapter 5 is adapted from "Beyond the Tax Effects in ESOP Financing," in the Spring 1988 issue of the *Journal of Applied Corporate Finance*. Finally, parts of Chapter 6 are adapted from two articles by John Kensinger and John Martin, with additional new material. These predecessors are "Project Financing: Raising Money the Old-Fashioned Way," published in the Fall 1988 issue of the *Journal of Applied Corporate Finance*, and "Project

Financing for Research and Development," published in *Research in Finance*, Vol. 8 (JAI Press, 1990). We are therefore deeply indebted to our colleague, John D. Martin, as well as the editors and reviewers of these articles.

We are also indebted to many of our friends and colleagues who have inspired and encouraged us to do research in these important and interesting areas in the past several years. Last, but not least, we would like to thank Susanne Dougherty who has tirelessly typed and retyped the manuscript.

NOTE

1. Reprinted from *Business Horizons*, November-December issue. Copyright 1989 by the Foundation for the School of Business at Indiana University. Used with permission.

Chapter 1

Introduction

In the wake of the revolution in corporate finance that occurred in the eighties, traditional concepts of corporate debt and equity no longer adequately describe the full array of financial arrangements. On one hand, new hybrids are being developed along several lines, all of which combine the attributes of debt and equity. On the other hand, new organizational forms are being devised that either limit lenders' recourse to the assets and cash flows of a specific project within a firm or convey an equity stake in a specific piece of the corporate pie. Therefore, a traditionalistic interpretation of the decade's apparently increased dependence upon debt financing can be very misleading.

There has been a rapid blurring of the distinction between debt and equity. Innovators have sometimes devised arrangements that combine the attributes of both debt and equity in efforts to create "tax-deductible equity" designed to reduce corporate income tax payments while retaining the flexibility of equity or to impose the constraints of debt upon managers while providing mechanisms for relaxing the constraints under certain circumstances that preserve some of the forgiveness of equity. In addition, the eighties have witnessed increased use of limited-recourse debt and the introduction of common stock with its risk reduced by a money-back guarantee. Such hybrids form a class of claims that cannot adequately be described as either debt or equity, but are better understood as "dequity."

Much of the debt piled up in the eighties has been part of a growing movement toward employee ownership of corporate stock. Perhaps the most widely familiar are the leveraged buyouts (LBOs), such as the firm of Kohlberg Kravis Roberts accomplished with Beatrice Foods or RJR Nabisco, in which a few senior executives obtained substantial ownership stakes in their companies. Leveraged employee stock ownership plans (LESOPs) have been less in the limelight, but more important in terms of their potential to effect significant changes in the nature of the workplace and the competitiveness of U.S. companies. The heavy doses of debt used to accomplish these changes in the structure of corporate ownership expose the lenders to much of the risk traditionally associated with equity investments. Yet these creditors have much to say about corporate financial decisions, making them seem more like stockholders than creditors. Furthermore, when such debt is held by tax-exempt institutional investors, large chunks of the corporate cash flows are no longer exposed to corporate income taxation.

HIGH-YIELD DEBT

Many are still perplexed by the rapid growth of the new market in bonds that were originally issued with ratings below investment grade. Explanations often move quickly to a listing of the alleged benefits for new businesses that would, it is said, otherwise have a hard time finding access to capital. In perfect capital markets, of course, the packaging doesn't matter. Companies with worthwhile potential could sell stock rather than lament their lack of an investment-grade bond rating. In an imperfect capital market in which a significant portion of capital is controlled by regulated financial institutions, however, the access-to-capital argument may have substance. High-yield bonds, particularly those with stock-purchase warrants or conversion options, offer an investment opportunity that institutions can label as debt for regulatory purposes but that has a significant equity component.

Regulators and their charges play a game that has sometimes been called the "regulatory dialectic," and banks have played it throughout the era of regulated banking since 1933. The game is simple: Regulators make rules intended to constrain the behavior of banks, but banks search imaginatively for loopholes in the rules. Then regulators respond by attempting to plug the most noisome loopholes, and the game starts anew. The recent experience with so-called "junk bonds" is an example of the regulatory dialectic at work and also provides a lesson in how to tell when something called debt is really dequity. In the case of junk bonds, a debt/equity hybrid was used to advance the regulatory dialectic to a new stage in its unfolding.

Under the limitations imposed by the Glass-Steagall Act, commercial banks were not allowed to take equity positions in their clients—banks could only lend. Yet, it is all too easy for a borrower to promise to repay an amount that is likely to be beyond its means. From the lender's perspective, surprisingly, this may be just fine. Two simple conditions are required to make the lender happy with the situation: The interest must be high enough to justify the risk, and the lender's portfolio of high-risk loans must be diversified. Just as a wildcat driller need not strike oil in every well, a lender in the high-yield market need not be repaid fully for every loan in order to earn a satisfactory return on the total portfolio of investments. Junk bonds offered the high yield, but more importantly, enhanced opportunity to diversify across many companies and regions.

As Black and Cox have demonstrated using the contingent-claims analysis, junior debt behaves partly like a senior bond and partly like a common stock. Thus, high yield contains a significant equity component. It is a dequity and could be called a "junk stock." To the buyers of high-yield bonds this has meant, not only higher risk, but higher potential reward. If the borrower performs well, the lender receives a high investment return from the premium interest rate and has the opportunity to exercise conversion privileges of the convertible bonds. If the borrower performs poorly, he would be caught in the debt trap and the lenders could become the "bondmailer" and get the company. For instance, Donald Trump in November 1990 handed over half of his ownership of the Taj Mahal (a casino in Atlantic City, New Jersey) to its bondholders after missing a $47.3 million interest payment. On both the upside and the downside, the outcome from investing in such bonds is little different from a straightforward equity investment—except that one is within the rules and the other is not. Prevented by regulation from making explicit equity investments, many bankers leaped through the loophole offered by bonds that were called debt but were really much like equity.

Many have condemned the banks for buying junk bonds or chided the regulators for allowing it. Some have even attacked the major figures in this multibillion-dollar market. It is not the intention here to resolve the issue of what banks should or should not be allowed to do. Like it or not, the regulatory dialectic is a fact of life. This round of it has finally played out to the point that limits have been imposed on the proportion of a financial institution's portfolio that can be held in the form of non-investment-grade bonds, resulting in forced sales of bonds as banks comply. Yet in the aftermath the environment is less restrictive than it was before the regulatory limits were pressed.

DEQUITY: HYBRIDS THAT ARE PART DEBT AND PART EQUITY

The legal distinction between debt and equity is vague. Moreover, concern about the distinction is primarily associated with income tax matters and resolution of bankruptcy claims, or arises from the efforts of regulators to police the activities of financial intermediaries. Prior to 1969 in the United States, the courts ruled on the distinction between what is debt and what is equity on a case-by-case basis. Because this approach proved to be unwieldy, the Tax Reform Act of 1969 empowered the Treasury Department to issue regulations "to determine whether an interest in a corporation is to be treated as stock or indebtedness" (Section 385). The Treasury Department finally issued its regulations in

1980, but they were withdrawn in 1983 because of the perception that any attempt at broad definition provides too many loopholes. (Several hybrid securities that were designed to take advantage of these regulations are discussed later in the book.) Once again, the question of whether a contract is debt or equity is being decided by the courts on a case-by-case basis.

Since the concept of debt implies a promise of some given amount of money to be repaid, which is enforceable by the courts, a contract that is vague or of questionable enforceability does not seem to qualify. Yet a firm may enter into a contract in which it promises to repay an amount that is likely to be beyond its means, for an appropriately small immediate consideration. The specificity of the promise makes it look like a debt arrangement. The great likelihood that the company will default and simply pay whatever it can, however, makes the arrangement look more like equity. When, then, does debt become equity? In the wake of the huge market for junk bonds in the late 1980s, this question is more than merely hypothetical. Indeed, there is no clear line drawn in the sand. Instead, there are a variety of instances in which securities have some aspects of debt, along with some aspects of equity.

There is more yet—dequity can be a still more complex concoction. Oliver Williamson used the term "dequity" in his 1988 article on corporate governance to refer, not only to a new financial instrument, but to a new governance structure that imposes a unique set of rules upon corporate management. In describing this creature, he wrote, "Let this instrument include all of the constraining features of debt. When, however, these constraints get in the way of value-maximizing activities, the board of directors (or some similar high-level oversight unit) can temporarily suspend the constraints."[1] Dequity is thus restrictive, but selectively so.

Perhaps the board of directors is not the best group to control the suspension of the constraints. The essence of investing in corporate stock is captured in the U.S. Supreme Court's 1946 decision in the case of *SEC v. W. J. Howey Co.*[2] In its decision, the court defined a security as "A contract, transaction, or scheme whereby a person invests his money in a common enterprise and is led to expect profits solely from the efforts of the promoter or third party." In the traditional corporate venture, that is, the investor's fate is virtually entirely in the hands of someone else. With dequity, however, the investors can provide safeguards to protect their interests. With dequity, an investor has more than a vote at the annual meeting as a means of directly influencing management action.

Investors can use dequity creatively when they want to impose restrictions on management discretion but at the same time want to specify conditions under which the constraints are automatically lifted or provide themselves with the means to make such choices under prespecified conditions. Therefore, the creation of dequity in all its varieties can involve a great deal more than merely creating a tax dodge, although it sometimes is just that. Dequity can also be more than a means for solving case-specific problems, although it is also sometimes just that, as well. In the broader sense, dequity can be the mechanism for defining new forms of business organization that are very different from the traditional corporation. Consider some specific forms of dequity that have recently had significant impact.

THE HIGH COST OF GOING PUBLIC AND SOME INNOVATIVE SOLUTIONS

The first great milestone on the entrepreneur's path is achieved when the new company makes its initial public offering of stock (IPO). The bad news associated with an IPO is the high cost. In addition to the underwriting fees paid to the investment banker, the stock sold in an IPO is, on average, underpriced by about 18 percent (for IPOs of all sizes). The problem is much worse for small IPOs (under $10 million), for which the average cost in fees and underpricing approaches 35 percent of the face value of the issue.

One potential explanation for the high cost of going public is the expense investors must incur to become well informed about the fledgling company. They will pay the price of becoming informed only in anticipation of a sufficiently large expected profit. To overcome this problem, innovators have experimented with arrangements that reduce the downside risk normally associated with equity investments by providing a "money-back guarantee." In such arrangements, common stockholders are divided into two groups, which face different risk/reward profiles. The new investors buy "units" composed of a share of common stock and a "right" provided by the issuing corporation. The right entitles the unit-holder to claim more stock if the market price of the stock falls below a stated level.

At a predetermined time, say at the end of two years, the issuer guarantees to support a floor value for each unit-holder's position. In the event that the market value of the company's stock has risen above the stated floor value, nothing happens. If the market value of the stock has fallen below the floor, however, the issuer is obligated to make up the difference by giving unit-holders additional common shares. (For example, if the market value of the company's stock were $10 per share at the maturity date of the right and the guaranteed floor were $15, the rights would entitle their holders to claim 50 new shares of common stock for every 100 rights they held.) Stock with a money-back guarantee allows the new investors to participate fully in the upside potential of a company with reduced downside risk. Thus, a stock with money-back guarantee, or the so-called "puttable stock," is a close substitute for convertible debt.

The simple expedient of equity with a money-back guarantee was pioneered in 1984 by Arley Merchandise Company, a small New England maker of custom draperies and upholstery. Having just won a large contract to supply a major hotel chain, it needed to boost its equity capital and sought to accomplish an initial placement of $6 million worth of stock. Because the company was still an unknown, however, Arley's owners could not persuade an investment banker to underwrite the stock at a price that was acceptable to them. They wanted at least $8 per share, but the investment banker believed $6 was as high as the public market would go. A solution was found by offering the new equity in "units" consisting of a share of stock plus a money-back guarantee (or put option) that would allow the investor to sell the stock back to the company on the second anniversary of the initial offering, for the original price. The units were offered at $8 each in November 1984, and the stock began trading on the American Stock Exchange, sans puts, in December. Thereupon, just as the investment banker had predicted, the price quickly stabilized at $6 per share. The Boston Stock Exchange, meanwhile, made a market in the separated puts and the whole units.

Through their willingness to lay themselves on the line in order to protect the initial buyers of the stock, Arley's original owners translated their confidence in the company's prospects into a higher stock price, overcoming the underpricing problem for their IPO. Their story ended happily, too, for the stock was trading at $10 by the time the second anniversary arrived, and no one asked for their money back.

Part of the high cost of going public may also arise from the underwriter's need to meet the "due diligence" rules established by the Securities Act of 1933. These rules mean that the underwriter must not only incur the cost of becoming informed about the fledgling company but also face the threat of a lawsuit from disgruntled stockholders if the fledgling fails. The underwriter, then, is offering a kind of "soft" money-back guarantee already. To collect such a guarantee from the underwriter, however, stockholders must prove in court that the underwriter was insufficiently diligent in its analysis. Given the high costs and risks involved in winning such a case, therefore, it stands to reason that a straightforward guarantee should have clear advantages.

Another recent development seemingly strengthens the prospects for making a money-back guarantee work. The obvious drawback in a situation like Arley's is that the guarantee is not backed by a strong, well-known entity. A solution is to arrange for a major bank to back the guarantee by issuing an irrevocable letter of credit (for a fee, of course). This was done in a June 1988 equity offering, with the guarantee backed by Citibank. Such an arrangement takes advantage of the bank's economies of scale in information processing, which can reduce the cost of becoming informed. Then, based on its analysis, the bank can assess an appropriate fee for extending the protection of its guarantee to the investors. With the analysis of fledgling companies now open to competition from commercial banks, there would seem to be new hope that the costs of going public will be reduced, as well as the uncertainties faced by investors.

Although it seems that an equity solution has been found for an important problem of raising the required additional capital, many fledgling companies have been equally satisfactory through mezzanine loans or other debt arrangements that include warrants or conversion options. For them, these alternatives have been more cost-effective than public stock offerings as a means for gaining an expanded equity base. (Later in the book it will be shown that stock with a money-back guarantee is nearly equivalent to mezzanine loans or convertible bonds.) These established alternatives have been widely used, whereas the so-called "equity" solution remains a rarity.

DEQUITY THAT TRANSFORMS EMPLOYEES INTO OWNERS

The Tax Reform Acts of 1984 and 1986 greatly strengthened the advantages of selling stock to an employee stock ownership plan (ESOP), including the following: (1) dividends paid on an ESOP's stock are tax-deductible for the corporation; (2) a financial institution that lends money to an ESOP pays tax on only half of the interest income; and (3) a company founder who sells stock to an ESOP can defer income tax on the capital gain if the profits are reinvested within a specified period. Encouraged by these incentives, in addition to the desire for increased productivity, 8,000 companies have formed ESOPs to purchase large blocks of their outstanding stock, using borrowed funds. Most of these are small companies, and many of them have never gone public. For these small firms in particular, the ESOP legislation provides a much-needed opportunity for the founders to "cash in" at the end of a successful career without incurring the high cost of an IPO. Not only the founders then gain the advantage of a diversified portfolio to provide a more secure retirement, but the employees get a chance to become the owners of their company.

Through leveraged buyouts, furthermore, many corporations have replaced their public equity with high-yield debt. Thus a significant portion of the increased debt burden that U.S. corporations have taken on has arisen through transactions that transform employees into the ultimate residual claimants. In the case of LBOs as well as ESOPs, the time-consuming and expensive bankruptcy procedures are being supplemented by private arbitration and out-of-court settlement. If the firm does poorly, the debt-holders get an increased proportion of the firm. In this regard, the "debt" in such arrangements is like equity with a money-back guarantee.

CLAIMS UPON SPECIFIC SLICES OF THE CORPORATE PIE

New Development in Limited-Recourse Debt

Many companies are using limited-recourse debt to finance a variety of activities, including inventory acquisition, plant construction, and development of mineral resources. Since these arrangements limit lenders' recourse to the assets and cash flows of specific projects, such debt offers the borrower many of the advantages traditionally associated with equity financing.

These limited-recourse arrangements are called "project financing" because an individual venture stands alone as an independent entity. Cash flows are paid out to the investors as they are earned, rather than reinvested in new projects in the same company, and the legal entity set up to establish the project has a finite life. The creditors have recourse only to the assets and cash flows of the project itself, without further recourse to the owners. The use of debt in project financing is thus comparable to the issuance of revenue bonds by a municipality, with payments restricted to the proceeds from a particular set of user fees or tax revenues,[3] and a project's viability as an independent financial entity likewise depends upon the "credit substance" behind the projected revenue stream.

Far from being a johnny-come-lately gimmick that has yet to stand the test of time, venture-by-venture financing of finite-lived projects has ancient roots, and was the rule in commerce until the nineteenth century.[4] Project-specific financial arrangements did not die with the industrial revolution but continued to be used through the years by European financiers for separately account-able ventures, such as overseas mineral exploration projects. In the continual experimentation to find the most efficient financial arrangements, project financing is once again finding widespread use. It is becoming increasingly common for corporations to establish individual projects as separate, finite-lived entities. From January 1, 1981 through September 31, 1990, underwriters have announced over $67 billion worth of project financings—an amount of financing equivalent to the formation of a new company in the upper echelon of the *Fortune* 500. The average of $835 million in announced project financings per month during 1988 and 1989 compares with an average of $30.2 billion per month of new securities (both debt and equity) issued by all U.S. corporations (sources: IDD Information Services, Inc., U.S. Securities and Exchange Commission, and the Board of Governors of the Federal Reserve System). Given that many project financings are not advertised by their underwriters, it is evident that project financing deserves to be taken seriously.

Project financing is being used extensively, not only to fund real estate development and oil and gas exploration, but independent electric power generation facilities, factories, and research and development efforts. During the eighties a vigorous market in the private placement of limited-recourse project financing has confronted financial managers in several industries with the decision of whether to make project financing arrangements or raise the funds for a project on the parent's own account. Project financing has become widespread among companies in oil and gas production, refining, gas transmission, chemicals, food processing, and textiles. (Later in the book a detailed look is taken at how this dequity solution solves some vexing business problems.)

R&D Limited Partnership

R&D partnerships are joint ventures or other temporary liaisons formed for the purpose of conducting the research necessary to develop a specific product, and their use has grown rapidly in the 1980s. They have been used by such companies as Genentech, Nova Pharmaceuticals, Amgen, and Cummins Engine. For example, when Cummins Engine needed to fund its research effort on a new generation of hybrid diesel engines (combining ceramic turbines and pistons as sources of power in a single powerplant), it used R&D limited partnership (RDLP) financing to raise $20 million for the project. Genentech's clinical partnerships likewise financed research into anticancer agents as well as human and animal growth hormones.

The use of RDLP financing by a variety of companies has grown rapidly since the first one was formed in 1978, opening a valuable new vehicle for channeling funds into the search for innovation. The U.S. Department of Commerce reported $1.7 billion of RDLP financing from 1978 to 1984 (involving more than 30 individual projects, plus several pools). From 1984 through 1989, one can document another $2.4 billion. (*Wall Street Journal*, March 10, 1986, p. 12; and Chen, Kensinger, and Martin, 1990). Although the tax reforms of 1984 and 1986 ended some abuses involving RDLPs, Robert A. Stanger Associates (a rating agency for limited partnerships) reports substantial recent growth in RDLP financing. Nor has the Revenue Enhancement Act of 1987 squelched investors' desire to own a piece of the action in high-tech research.

Merrill Lynch, Prudential-Bache, Paine Webber, and Morgan Stanley, moreover, are actively involved in R&D efforts through RDLP pools under their management. Merrill Lynch, for example, has formed a subsidiary, Merrill Lynch R&D Management, which serves as general partner in its RDLPs. In-house expertise is provided by two vice-presidents with technical backgrounds. One is a Ph.D. chemist who was formerly director of corporate R&D at a major pharmaceuticals company, and the other has his Ph.D. in electrical engineering.

The R&D management company is responsible, not only for managing the projects of the partnership, but for selecting them. In finding projects, it focuses on small companies, including startups, that have already developed base technologies and have reached the stage at which second-round financing is needed to develop patentable products. The partnership then pays a licensing fee for the use of the base technology and hires the innovator to conduct the remaining research. The resulting patents belong to the partnership, which also receives the option to buy common stock in the corporations with which it goes into business (so it has a stake in their other activities as well). Finally, the R&D management company arranges strategic manufacturing/marketing partnerships when such capabilities are lacking in the companies conducting the research.

Merrill Lynch R&D Management Company is very much involved in the process of initiating and conducting research efforts, but it differs from a traditional corporation in some very important ways. The RDLP it manages has a finite life, and all of its capital is equity, unlike most corporations on both counts. The partnership agreement states that it will terminate not later than January 31, 2005 (at which time it would be only 19 years old) but plans are to terminate it at the age of ten. If new backers can be found for follow-on partnerships, the process will continue, but there is no provision for automatic roll-over of proceeds from old ventures into new ones. In the meantime, however, the backers are fully committed to their projects: Pulling out early is difficult, not only for individual partners, but also for the partnership as a whole. Thus, this pool of pure equity qualifies eminently for recognition as the kind of "patient capital" said to be lacking in American enterprise today.

Merrill Lynch closed its first ML Technology Ventures partnership in September 1985, and by spring 1988 had committed the entire $70 million to projects at 14 different companies. Seven of them introduced new products in 1988. Another $80 million Merrill Lynch RDLP closed in September 1988. Paine Webber closed its second $80 million RDLP in early 1988. Prudential-Bache has been regularly acquiring new funds each quarter for the last two years in its series of Pru-Tech partnerships and has raised about $200 million so far.

Through such arrangements a large corporation with strengths in manufacturing or marketing can profit from liaisons with small, nimble, low-cost organizations that can develop new products and technologies but lack the capability to follow through on their own. For instance, Motorola has developed strategic partnerships with several small but well-established makers of equipment used in the production and testing of semiconductors. Rather than trying to develop an in-house capability to produce such machines, Motorola strives to transfer internally generated concepts for innovative equipment to its partners, who in turn develop the concepts into working machines. Once specifications are agreed upon, Motorola issues a purchase order, and the strategic partners arrange their own financing. Armed with their purchase orders, the contractors (most of whom are not publicly held) have the option of obtaining large-scale financing without expanding their equity base. The lenders have no recourse to Motorola should a contractor not be able to deliver. Motorola, moreover, need not arrange financing until the working machinery is ready. Thus the risks associated with progressing from concept to factory floor are transferred away from the sponsor, making it easier for the engineers to gain consent from corporate headquarters.

Other New Development in Limited Partnership Financing for New Technology

Recent experiments with partnership forms of organization may be laying the foundations of a new alternative for organizing economic activity. Only time, of course, will tell the extent to which this alternative displaces integrated corporations. In this alternative investors still enjoy limited liability but relinquish much less power to managers. Investors are the direct recipients of cash flows from mature operations. They are then free to choose whether or not they wish to provide funding for the development of new products by participating in R&D partnerships. If development efforts are successful, the partnership's rights may be sold or licensed to a manufacturer/marketer. Alternatively, investors may choose to participate in manufacturing and marketing by means of other partnerships.

Recently, with strong encouragement and support from the U.S. Department of Commerce, a few firms have experimented with limited partnerships formed for the purpose of promoting and marketing a specific product. Bruce Merrifield, assistant secretary of commerce for productivity, technology, and innovation during the Reagan Administration, threw the resources of the Commerce Department behind an effort to help in overcoming the initial barriers to forming partnerships for the purpose of manufacturing and marketing specific products. Energy Sciences Corporation offers an example. It developed a data networking system that sends data via low-frequency radio signals over existing phone or power lines, while leaving normal utility services undisturbed. The development was financed largely with RDLPs. Then the company's marketing campaign was financed by what it calls "technology marketing partnerships."[5]

These marketing partnerships are in essence very simple. They are business organizations formed for the purpose of bringing a specific product or group of products to market. The general partner may manufacture the product or contract it to a third party. The general partner also contracts with third parties for advertising and promotion. The partnership owns the trademark and brandname supported by its advertising and has an exclusive distributorship for the product. It earns revenues from royalties or commissions paid out of sales by the manufacturer. In some cases they are set up with an option for the manufacturer to buy out the distributorship for a lump sum. Thus, each partnership is a network organization, similar to the model exemplified by the sports shoe marketer Nike (which, although it is a corporation, serves as a good example of such a network hub). Nike contracts its manufacturing to offshore factories, itself serving as developer and marketer of products. Partnerships can function in this role just as well as corporations can, but with a product-specific lifespan and less management discretion over reinvestment of cash flows.

There can be great tax advantages generated by these arrangements, but they also provide a project-specific organizational alternative to the integrated corporation. It is possible for a product to be developed by a partnership and brought to market by another partnership, with heavy reliance upon capital raised in the public market. In such a complex of small, specialized organizations the primary role of managers is to run existing operations efficiently. In order to increase the assets under their management, they have to compete by creating alluring new opportunities to be offered in the marketplace for capital.

In such networks of partnership financing the work would be done by professional firms (much like law firms or accounting firms) specializing in research, product design, or marketing. Manufacturing would be contracted out to offshore factories or to flexible automated factories near the final market. Finally, the key role of pulling all the pieces together could go to a new breed of investment banker.

Master Limited Partnerships

In some cases the limited partners' shares, called "units," can be bought and sold. Such limited partnerships are often referred to as master limited partnerships, and several are listed on the New York Stock Exchange. Unlike common stock, however, the market value of partnership units is expected to decline as the lifespan of the partnership draws to a close. Investors buy them for their cash flows rather than for anticipated price increases.

Active trading of limited partnership units need not necessarily jeopardize the tax status of the partnership, because this alone will not cause it to be treated as a corporation for tax purposes. Tax law allows a duly constituted limited partnership to be treated as such so long as it does not have more of the characteristics of a corporation than of a partnership. The determination is made by the answers to four questions. If the answer is yes to more than two of them, the partnership is taxed as a corporation. The questions are as follows (see 26CFR 301.7701-2.):

- Does the partnership have continuity of life?
- Is there centralization of management in the partnership?
- Is there limited liability for all members of the partnership?
- Do all partners have free transferability of partnership interests?

When partnership units are traded publicly, the answer to the last question is not necessarily yes. If only the limited partners have the power of substituting someone else for themselves in the partnership, but one of the general partners does not, the attribute of free transferability may not be judged to be present. Furthermore, even if the answer to the last question were "yes," an answer of "no" on at least two others would preserve partnership tax treatment. The third question will rate a "no" so long as the general partner bears full liability for the obligations of the partnership, and Treasury regulations contain detailed guidelines for making this determination. The partnership will usually be judged not to have continuity of life as long as it is set up so that at least one member (a general partner) is crucial to its survival. Only if the partnership were set up so that it could survive the death or bankruptcy of the general partner would continuity of life normally be judged to be present. Finally, limited partners are not expected to have any involvement in management. Therefore, as long as the general partner is diligently involved as manager, centralization of management would not normally be judged to be present.

The IRS often won't give guarantees about tax treatment before an investment is made in a limited partnership, so there is risk that favorable tax treatment might be denied after the fact. Nevertheless, it is possible to put together a variety of reasonable, arms-length arrangements that are within the spirit of the partnership laws and that have a high probability of being treated as such by the tax authorities. Certainly it is possible for such arrangements to include liquidity for the limited partners via securitization of their partnership units.

Corporate Hollowing

Limited-recourse debt or other forms of project financing are not the only means to use dequity in a way that achieves a significant change in the relationship between investors and managers. Increasingly, investors prefer to own airplanes instead of stock in airline companies, oil wells instead of stock in integrated oil companies, timberlands instead of stock in forest products companies, and real estate instead of corporate stock. They often do so by means of financial arrangements that utilize dequity financing, such as limited partnerships, limited-recourse debt, or limited-recourse leases. Such uses of dequity are part of a migration of business activities to new organizational forms that give investors more control over management. The most visible manifestation of this trend is the so-called "hollowing" or "downsizing" of corporations as investors increasingly retain title to working assets.

The downsizing trend has been facilitated by the growing practice of securitizing specialized pools of assets. For example, it is now commonplace for financial institutions to sell insured mortgages in the form of securities. Credit card receivables, auto and truck loans are likewise packaged into high-denomination securities for resale. In addition there are hundreds of limited partnerships that own oil and gas wells, hydro, geothermal, and cogeneration power production facilities, oil refineries, and even factories, as well as timberland properties, cable television systems, real estate, mortgages, restaurant services, and mortgage loan servicing. All sorts of income-producing operations that require little more than caretaker management have been organized as partnerships or other independent entities and funded through limited-recourse project financings. Even management-intensive operations, such as R&D projects, have been financed as separate organizational entities.

Part of the motivation is that income taxation at the corporate entity level can be eliminated when assets are owned directly by individuals or tax-exempt institutional investors. The corporation then pays rent for the use of the assets, with full deduction as business expenses. Even though the investors or the recipients of retirement income from a pension fund pay individual taxes on the resulting income, taxation is eliminated at the level of the corporate entity.

Besides the tax advantages, however, there is another important additional effect, in the form of increased managerial accountability. The sale of a corporation's real estate holdings to a trust or limited partnership, for example, or the decision to lease rather than buy equipment such as ships, aircraft, or factories, can be a particularly potent step in the process of returning resource-allocation decisions to the marketplace. When it owned the property, the corporation might weather a bad year or two without having to confess that it was losing money. Without the necessity of writing rent checks, the management could ignore the fact that the company was not earning enough to justify the space it occupied. After the sale of the company's real estate, though, management would have to give an accounting if the company could not pay its rent.

So dequity sometimes provides the means for solving case-specific problems or reducing taxes, but the creation of dequity in all its varieties can involve a great deal more. In the broader sense, dequity can be the mechanism for defining new forms of business organization that are very different from the traditional corporation. Through these arrangements corporations as we now know them dwindle in importance, while investors increasingly become direct owners of working assets. Lower capital costs can be achieved by leasing equipment instead of owning it, as well as buying inputs and components from networks of small, employee-owned facilities.

NOTES

1. See Oliver Williamson, "Corporate Finance and Corporate Governance," p. 581.

2. *SEC v. W. J. Howey Co.*, 328 U.S. 293, 298, 299 (1946).

3. When the revenues to be derived from a new municipal project offer more stability than the general revenues of a municipality, the cost of capital can be reduced by isolating the project from the general pool. Given the political hurdles to overcome in making a project happen, the ability to point to a low cost of capital can be a selling point (even if, theoretically, the low-risk project would reduce the municipality's overall cost of capital).

4. For a summary of the early history of project financing and the reasons for its period of quiescence, see John Kensinger and John Martin, "Project Financing: Raising Money the Old-Fashioned Way," pp. 69–81.

5. For more details, see *Financial Planning*, pp. 181–88.

REFERENCES

Black, Fischer, and John Cox. "Valuing Corporate Securities: Some Effects of Bond Indenture Provisions," *Journal of Finance*, May 1976, pp. 351–67.

Chen, Andrew, John Kensinger, and John Martin. "Project Financing as a Means for Preserving Financial Flexibility," Working Paper, April 1990.

Financial Planning, October 1985, pp. 181–88.

Kensinger, John, and John Martin. "Project Financing: Raising Money the Old-Fashioned Way," *Journal of Applied Corporate Finance*, Vol. 1, No. 3 (Fall 1988), pp. 69–81.

Wall Street Journal, March 10, 1986, p. 12.

Williamson, Oliver. "Corporate Finance and Corporate Governance," *Journal of Finance*, 63, July 1988, pp. 567–91.

Chapter 2

Dequity: The Restrictions of Debt with the Flexibility of Equity

Every individual, therefore, endeavors as much as he can both to employ his capital in the support of domestic industry, and so to direct that industry that its produce may be of the greatest value . . . and he is in this, as in many other cases, led by an invisible hand to promote an end which was no part of his intention.

—Adam Smith, 1776[1]

Dequity can be more than a tool for creating tax-deductible equity, however. Nor is it just a way of solving case-specific income problems. Indeed, many of the debt/equity hybrids accomplish a significant change in the rules that govern management behavior, making management more accountable to investors and giving investors more control over the cash flows of the enterprise. When properly constructed, however, a dequity financing lets investors suspend or alter the restrictions on corporate management if warranted by a change in the business environment. Moreover, what transpires is just a new chapter in the age-old power struggle between managers and investors.

The noise and thunder of front-page press and congressional debate have surrounded the behavior and the economic welfare contributions of the corporate junk bond dealers and the corporate control raiders; but without fanfare and glaring lights, other market forces are accomplishing a quiet restructuring with far-reaching consequences. In a play on the words of Adam Smith, the raiders have been "the visible foot" because they bring about change by force.[2] No one likes to be kicked around, though, so the raiders have many enemies. Even if the raiders were to disappear, however, there would still be "the invisible hand" of the marketplace to quietly encourage corporate restructuring and downsizing, enticing rather than forcing.

The variety of opportunities offered in today's financial marketplace is unprecedented. For an entrepreneur just setting out, there are venture capitalists and business incubators to help in the birthing process. For a vigorous technology startup company there are billions of dollars available through mezzanine loans, joint ventures, project financing, and public stock offerings. For an established corporate giant there are not only concerns about hostile takeovers and flak from militant stockholders but also attractive opportunities, such as converting the treasury function into a profit center through vigorous securities trading and international financial arbitrage or securitizing assets and turning them into ready cash. Then, too, there is the appealing prospect of advancing the management team members' own individual self-interest by arranging a leveraged buyout.

The good news is that the financial markets have evolved to a point where capital can flow quickly to enable brand-new companies to develop new products and technologies. Some of this money, however, flows as a result of cutting big companies apart and wringing cash out of declining operations. When the money from these sometimes painful actions reaches investors, they decide where to reinvest in new businesses. Established tradition, in contrast, is for large companies to remove resources from the marketplace and substitute management fiat for the invisible hand in directing the flow of capital from the old to the new.

Not long ago it was widely accepted that an ideal corporation consisted of a portfolio of projects at various stages of development, which was balanced so that the cash flows from the mature activities were used to nourish fledgling projects. In the parlance of the Boston Consulting Group, the "cash cows" were milked to feed the "rising stars." As they grew old, cash cows became "dogs," and were harvested to feed more rising stars for the company. Over this menagerie stood the corporate managers who did strategic planning, deciding which new projects to finance. If their own organization was not generating enough cash to support its rising stars, they would even go out into the market to buy someone else's cash cow. If, on the other hand, they had lots of cash cows but too few deserving new projects, they might buy another company's rising star.

This approach did not stand the test of time, however, because today's investors have a much broader spectrum of opportunities than do corporate managers who have set a goal of investing internally. Stockholder discontent with the old model helped fuel the recent wave of corporate takeovers. Simply put, the investors declared their preference to milk the cash cows themselves. Now, through various means for limiting management discretion over the reinvestment of corporate cash flows, the give and take of the marketplace is creating a new kind of cash cow. The cash flow from mature operations is being channeled back into the marketplace for reinvestment—often in unknown startups.

Ironically, the invisible hand nudges management into voluntarily releasing control over resource-allocation decisions in a variety of ways. Even though this process may not be part of a conscious intention, it leads to better resource allocation and boosts America's competitiveness. Investors flush with cash flowing from mature operations now have a variety of opportunities to underwrite new growth. Investors, in fact, frequently have a far more sumptuous array of such choices in the marketplace than do corporate managers seeking to reinvest internally. When investors get to choose the most attractive opportunities from the full capital market menu, therefore, financial resources are put to higher-valued uses than would be the case if managers made the decision within the narrower confines of their own firms.

WHY DEQUITY IS ATTRACTIVE TO INVESTORS

In the theory of the firm literature, there is a concept which says that the fundamental result of the formation of a firm is to remove resources from the control of markets and place them under the discretionary control of the firm's management. In a sense, then, the firm can be thought of as a competitor of the marketplace. The firm has even been characterized as a "mini capital market" wherein funds from a firm's operations are reallocated internally at the discretion of management.[3] The seed capital for the firm was originally acquired via market contracts with investors, of course, but their say in the reinvestment of internal funds flow is generally limited.

One way to characterize this situation is to say that capital is removed from the marketplace when the corporation issues new stock. It and all it produces are impounded within the firm for an indefinite period, to be returned only when management agrees. A reversal of this process, which returns capital to the control of the marketplace, might be called "unfirming" the firm.[4] There is a natural tension between the marketplace and firms—the marketplace tolerates firms only when there are benefits to be gained.

Why do investors allow so much discretion to managers? On the most basic level, it may simply be that investors cannot afford to control every detail of a business, and so delegate control to managers. R. M. Coase is credited with suggesting, half a century ago, that economies of scale in contracting for resources in the marketplace provide the incentive for the formation of firms.[5] That is, if investors were to maintain positive control over their businesses, they would have to specify their decisions in detailed contracts. Writing, monitoring, and enforcing such a set of highly specific contracts would be much more expensive than simply granting managers broad discretionary powers over the resources held by a firm.

As the contracting costs of direct market control fall and reduce the cost advantage of managerial discretion, investors demand more direct control over the use of resources bought with their money. The recent strengthening of spot markets in oil and the advent of futures contract trading on various oil products, for example, have diminished the economic role of the managements of large integrated oil companies. Now the marketplace plays a strong role in regulating the flow of oil—a role formerly played by the forward-contracting activities of major oil firms.

Even so, contracting costs explain why managers have control over operational matters but not why they have the first option to reinvest the firm's cash flow. An interesting alternative explanation for the existence of firms, however, can be gleaned from recent developments. Consider a firm that has a new technology to exploit. In order to obtain the necessary financing, the firm will need to locate interested investors and share sufficient information to entice them to finance the venture. The management is recognized by investors as having a vested interest in making the project sound as good as possible so that funding can be obtained under the most favorable terms (and consequently, as little of the value of the investment as possible will have to be shared with the new investors). Thus potential investors may view management's recommendations skeptically and will demand substantial amounts of verifiable information.

On the other hand, the management of the firm cannot reveal too many of the details of the venture without running the risk of valuable competitive secrets falling into the hands of its competitors. Thus the firm's management finds itself caught on the horns of a dilemma. In order to get the most favorable financing terms, management must reveal as much information as possible about the intended use of new funds. Not to reveal enough would result in a transfer of wealth from existing investors to the newcomers. Yet to do so would erode the firm's competitive advantage by revealing critical information to competitors. Firms may own significant proprietary information and have valuable investment opportunities that would be subject to loss of value if facts about them were revealed prematurely outside the firm.[6] Such firms will find that milking their own cash cows is the optimal solution, because then the funds can flow to the new projects without compromising vital competitive information.

If an organization runs out of natural growth opportunities when its industry matures, it no longer has such a need for cash cows. At this point investors legitimately demand a return of control to their own hands. When control over resource allocation is returned to the marketplace, the investors get to make all of the reinvestment decisions, because *they* have first claim to the cash flows. With cash in hand, investors can choose among venture capital funds, initial public offerings, real estate, energy exploration partnerships, R&D project pools, or any other profitable investment vehicle. Investors gain direct control over their money, and managers of corporations thereby give way to investment bankers in the role of guiding funds from the cash cows into the rising stars. Given that such control has market value, there is reason to believe that unfirming may enhance value.

Managers often resist, however, and try to perpetuate the firm. Why would managers try to keep the firm going beyond its useful life—past the point where it has an economic advantage that justifies its control over resources? Managers feel commitments to many other corporate stakeholders than the investors who contributed capital.[7] They are typically far closer to the corporation's employees, for example, than they are to the investors. Likewise, they feel closer ties to the community that houses the corporation than they do to a faceless and widely dispersed group of public investors.

It can be very difficult, therefore, for them to visualize a future in which their corporation does not exist in some form. After the purpose for which it was conceived has been served, there are still strong pressures, both emotional and political, to extend the firm's life by redirecting its resources into some new set of activities, even though they may not be the most highly valued use for the resources. Managers who are trying their best to be good citizens and to do what they perceive to be right for their employees and local communities may have interests that are very much at odds with those of investors and the economy at large. This sort of conflict can present some very thorny issues; but it ultimately leads to the question of whether to let the marketplace achieve the highest-valued uses for the world's resources or try to slow down progress and avoid making difficult decisions.

WHY DEQUITY IS ATTRACTIVE TO MANAGEMENT

Whoever has discretionary power over the reinvestment of its operating cash flows has fundamental power over the future of a firm. The extreme use of debt (in leveraged share repurchases, leveraged buyouts, and debt/equity swaps, for example) substantially erodes management power over the deployment of cash flows generated by a firm's mature operations. Consider the impact of leveraged share repurchases, such as the ones that T. Boone Pickens forced on Phillips Petroleum and Unocal. Something like it also happened with Gulf, in that Chevron borrowed heavily in order to buy out the Gulf stockholders. In all of these, the stockholders came away with a substantial wealth increase, in cash. It came in the form of capital gains for most of them, so the maximum tax rate anyone had to pay was 20 percent (these things happened, of course, before the Tax Reform Act of 1986). The shareholders were then free to choose how to reinvest this wealth, selecting from the full array of opportunities in the marketplace.

Where did this wealth increase for the stockholders come from? Much of it may have come from the tax benefits of leverage, but that is not the whole story. Besides any tax effect it might have, the leverage fundamentally altered the scope of management discretion. Michael Jensen recently coined the "free cash flow hypothesis" to explain this, and it goes as follows. With strong creditors to appease, the cash flows become committed to interest and debt retirement for a significant period into the future. New projects would have to compete for external funding, rather than be sustained by the cash flows from the oil fields. Besides the tax effect, then, dequity financing brings with it a change in the processes by which management actions are monitored and changes the way managers are motivated. The revised rules force the cash to flow out of the firm rather than circulate within it.

If there is any danger that management might not be as demanding in scrutinizing internal investments as the marketplace is, this change increases the probability that the cash flows will find their way to the highest-valued uses. After the leveraged share repurchases, there was much less of a chance that Phillips or Unocal might buy a Reliance Electric or a Montgomery Ward or a Kennecott Copper.[8] Nor would their managements be able to follow up on any temptation to get into the office products business, as did Exxon with such poor success. With cash flows committed to debt service, managers had their wings clipped and stockholders had their money. As one would expect, managers were less happy about it than were the stockholders.

Some people raise the concern that diverting cash flows from oil and gas production into the marketplace might be detrimental in the long run. That is, the oil may eventually be depleted without replacement of reserves. Phillips management, for example, lamented the impact of the "crushing mountain of debt" upon their exploration efforts, claiming that pleasing the financial marketplace requires short-run maximization of cash flows at the expense of long-run economic viability. The marketplace, however, is the ultimate source of resources for commitment to any venture. When the marketplace puts a high enough value on oil and gas exploration, new drilling partnerships can be formed quickly. Meanwhile, there are opportunities in electronics, robotics, artificial intelligence, and bioengineering (to name a few) that are more appealing to the marketplace. In fact, a recent study of the impact of new internal investments upon corporate stock values found strong evidence against what the Phillips managers were saying. The researchers found that on average (although certainly not in every case) announcements of capital expenditures by corporations resulted in increased stock values.[9]

LEVERAGED BUYOUTS AND EMPLOYEE
STOCK OWNERSHIP PLANS

What T. Boone Pickens did through leveraged share repurchases at Phillips Petroleum and Unocal, the firm of Kohlberg Kravis Roberts has done in other industries through LBOs. There have been many explanations offered for the LBO phenomenon, each of which may have some element of truth in it. Without offering a definitive explanation for all of them, however, it is possible to note the following common results:

1. Stockholders are able to sell their stock for cash, at a premium over the market value, and are immediately free to reinvest the cash in the most attractive opportunities available anywhere in the marketplace.

2. Managers gain a shot at ownership, and without changing jobs go to work for new bosses. They are free of the burden of reporting to a large group of public shareholders. In place of the shareholders, however, management must answer to the LBO specialist, whose group generally takes a strong position on the board of directors.

3. Finally, in place of a host of public shareholders demanding ever-increasing earnings and dividends, the managers have to placate a small group of creditors who demand that every stray penny be applied to a speedy repayment of the debt used to finance the buyout.

Whatever hypothesis one offers to explain why LBOs are happening, they have a common result. The decisions about how to reinvest the cash flows from the assets of the companies involved are transferred from corporate managers to the marketplace. In a buyout, then, managers do not escape monitoring; they merely exchange one form of monitoring for another. Nor do they escape pressure—in fact, it might seem that the pressure on them increases as a result of dequity financing. To be sure, they have the advantage that the bite taken from cash flows by income tax is reduced, giving them more to work with. They are not, however, "their own men" until the debt is taken care of. With cash flows committed to debt support, new projects will not have access to the milk from the old cash cow, and any growth plans must face the test of the marketplace.

Some people cry out that this stifles the economy, but it must not be forgotten that the stockholders got an infusion of cash at the very beginning. They will be reinvesting in growth opportunities elsewhere. In addition, the creditors of the newly private company will be receiving regular shipments of milk from the cash cow, which they will be able to reinvest in the best available opportunities. Only when the debt is repaid will the managers, at that point certainly older and perhaps wiser, once again have access to the cash spigot to finance internal expansion projects. Then it will be their own money they are spending, and they may be more demanding about the prospects for potential projects than when they were employees of a public corporation.

Besides the garden-variety LBO, there is another new player on the dequity scene. Leveraged employee stock ownership plans have been the vehicle for several buyouts recently. In these arrangements a special trust is formed to purchase stock and credit it to the accounts of individual employees. The Tax Reform Act of 1984 added two very attractive new sweeteners for leveraged ESOPs. Since January 1985, dividends paid to stock owned by an ESOP have been tax-deductible. In addition, lenders need pay income tax on only half of the interest paid to them by an ESOP. Thus ESOPs are able to borrow at low interest rates, in order to buy stock in the employer corporation. Finally, employer corporations are allowed to make tax-deductible contributions of cash or stock to ESOPs, and through 1987 may even earn tax credits in addition. With these incentives, an ESOP can borrow the money to finance a buyout of an employer's stock, with the employer's guarantee on the loan. Debt support payments would come from dividends and employer's cash contributions, so the entire amount—both principal and interest—can be tax-deductible.[10]

Through such an arrangement it is possible for the corporation to eliminate income tax completely and make the entire pretax cash flow of the corporation available for debt retirement. Only if the corporation retained earnings for new investment would there be any need to pay income tax—which is a significant turning of the tables. Not long ago, income tax laws had the effect of keeping cash inside a company since paying dividends resulted in double taxation. In the case of a buyout by a leveraged ESOP under current tax rules, the tax penalty is instead levied against retention of earnings for reinvestment. Instead of retaining earnings, then, the best way for an ESOP-owned corporation to raise expansion capital is by selling new stock to the ESOP; and when this requires the ESOP to go to the market for loans, the growth plans must meet outside scrutiny.

Besides giving employees a chance to own their companies, then, ESOPs do two other important things common to dequity financing. First, they put cash into the hands of stockholders, who then make the reinvestment decisions themselves. Second, leveraged ESOPs commit the firm's cash flows to debt retirement and divert the flow out of the cash cow back into the marketplace, where it can nourish the highest-valued new ventures.

THE MOTIVATION FOR CORPORATE HOLLOWING

There are several means available to "securitize" a specialized pool of assets. It is now commonplace for financial institutions to sell insured mortgages in the form of securities. Credit card receivables, auto and truck loans are likewise packaged into high-denomination securities for resale. Receivables can also be held by a corporation's financial subsidiary, and a portion of the subsidiary sold to the public. Whole divisions may also be set up as parent-controlled subsidiaries, with a portion of stock offered to the public.

In addition, there are now more than 90 master limited partnerships (MLPs) publicly traded. Originated in the oil and gas industry, they have spread to timberland properties, cable television systems, real estate, mortgages, restaurant services, and mortgage loan servicing. Nonlisted partnerships also own large-scale hydro and geothermal power generating plants, cogeneration facilities, and even oil refineries. All sorts of income-producing operations that require little more than care-taker management have been separated from a corporation, organized as a partnership, and sold. More management-intensive operations, such as R&D projects, have also been financed as separate projects.[11]

The choice of organizational form used for securitizing assets is sensitive to the tax environment. The 1987 Tax Act requires that publicly traded partnerships be taxed as corporations. In the absence of favored tax treatment for publicly traded partnerships, a corporate subsidiary or a nontraded partnership may be the organizational form chosen as the repository for the assets to be sold. One should not, however, give up on innovative financial professionals; on the real estate front, for example, they are turning once again to trusts. This continual give and take between innovative financial engineers and the taxing authorities reflects the "regulatory dialectic" at work—as fast as the authorities close one avenue, innovators find new ways to carry on.[12]

Managements of many large corporations have tasted the infusion of cash that comes from securitizing assets, perhaps without noticing an important side effect. The sale of a corporation's real estate holdings to a trust or limited partnership, for example, can be a particularly potent step in the process of returning resource-allocation decisions to the marketplace. When a company owns its operating space, it serves as its own land-lord—and part of its profit really represents rent. If the property is sold to a specialized subsidiary, two obvious things happen: the corporation's profit drops because it begins paying explicit rent, and the corporation's income tax drops accordingly. When the subsidiary is carefully constructed, its income escapes taxation at the corporate level. The tax consequences are the obvious effect, but something else happens that may not have been intended—the corporation becomes subject to eviction. When it owned the property, the corporation might weather a bad year or two without having to confess that it was losing money. Without the necessity of writing rent checks, the management might ignore the fact that the company was not earning enough to justify the space it occupied. After the sale of the company's real estate, however, the management would have to give an accounting if the company could not pay its rent.

In the traditional model of the corporation, managers are expected, not only to run existing operations efficiently, but to take primary responsibility for deciding how to reinvest the cash flows. They may decide to pay cash dividends, which the stockholders are then free to reinvest as they see fit, but managers have first crack at the money. When assets are sold to special-purpose subsidiaries, things often work on a different basis. These subsidiaries frequently involve high financial leverage and often utilize the limited partnership organizational form. Management is charged with the efficient operation of existing enterprises but has a restricted role in the reinvestment decisions, due to the necessity of making debt service payments. When limited partnership arrangements are used, the managing partner's discretion in dividend/reinvestment matters is restricted further, since revenues and expenses are credited directly to the partners' individual accounts according to a fixed contractual formula. Once the accounting decisions are made, the individual partners receive their pro rata share of the cash produced by the partnership assets, and the reinvestment decisions are their own.

Limited partnerships are very flexible organizational forms that convey to investors the corporate advantage of limited liability, but without double taxation (except when they are publicly traded). There is wide latitude possible in the terms that can be stated in the partnership agreement. After the agreement is entered into, however, the general partners' discretion over the use of partnership assets is bound by its terms. These partnerships are finite-lived, with a well-defined set of conditions for their demise. Although limited partnerships give up day-to-day control of the enterprise in exchange for limited liability, they still have access to the partnership ledgers to monitor compliance with the agreement and can vote in extraordinary circumstances (for example, the removal of a general partner). Furthermore, the partnership agreement spells out explicitly how the partnership profits are to be paid out to the partners.

In some cases, however, the general partner may enjoy considerable discretion in the early years of the partnership. T. Boone Pickens has even parlayed this kind of discretion into takeover attempts. For example, Mesa Partners II was the major stockholder in Unocal during the recent takeover attempt. Then in January 1986, Mesa Limited Partnership made a run at KN Energy, the Colorado-based natural gas concern. Typically, such partnerships are structured to take maximum advantage of the tax situation. By recomputing the tax basis of depletable properties, for example, the partnership may generate large losses in the early years. These losses are credited to the individual partners' accounts according to the partnership agreement. Subsequent profits must be credited up to a predefined point before cash payments begin to flow to limited partners. During the early years there may be substantial cash flows within the partnership over which the general partner exercises reinvestment discretion. As time passes, however, that discretion irresistibly erodes.

CORPORATIONS ARE BECOMING MORE LIKE BANKS

As a recent study noted, "The decisions made by corporate treasurers have a potential impact on corporate profits which is often as large as the earnings from operations."[13] At first this statement might conjure up images of bond refunding or treasury stock transactions, but there is much more involved. In a growing number of companies, the corporate treasury no longer serves simply as a means to raise funds in support of operations, and many financial executives are discovering the possibilities for making the treasury active as a profit center in securities trading.

In October 1984, for example, Exxon Capital Corporation (a wholly owned subsidiary of Exxon Corporation), issued twenty-year Eurobonds with principal of $1.8 billion and invested the proceeds in U.S. Treasury securities. The transaction was arranged in such a way that Exxon realized a substantial riskless profit after taxes, by taking advantage of tax differentials and international restrictions on capital flows.[14]

On the surface this seems rather unexceptional—no more nor less than an incursion by an oil company onto the turf of bankers—but it has an important hidden result. When the treasury is a profit center, alternative internal investments must compete with it for funding. As it grows, the trading function offers employment for more and more of the corporation's internal cash flow. Thus, potential investments in operations must compete with the array of opportunities in the full external capital market. If the rate of return for new plant or capital equipment, taking into account risk, is not competitive with outside investments, such internal projects will languish. This is, of course, how things are *supposed* to be in theory; but there needs to be a practical incentive to get it done. Aggressive outside investment by the treasury, with the potential of investing in the full range of opportunities available in the marketplace, is just such an incentive. A corporation can no longer go on functioning as a "mini capital market" once the treasury begins actively channeling funds into the external capital market.

THIS MOVEMENT IS PROPELLED BY OPPORTUNITIES IN NEW TECHNOLOGIES

The capital impounded in old-line corporations is needed elsewhere. Until recently, the large capital requirements and the tax structure gave big corporations a competitive advantage in the conduct of industrial research. With increased access to the capital markets, however, the brightest scientists and design engineers now have a very real option to leave the safety of a steady job in the research division of a large corporation and strike out on their own with new startup companies.

Major industrial research traditionally has been accomplished within the confines of large integrated corporations, financed by the cash flows from established operations. The idea of the product life cycle, which came into vogue some 60 years ago, provides the foundation for the traditional concept of an integrated corporation that exploits products through all phases of their life cycles. The heart of such a traditional integrated corporation is R&D. As old products decline so that reinvesting cash flows in the associated production processes no longer pays, the excess cash flow is channeled to research and development of new products; thus, there is continual renewal.

Entrepreneurship, however, can be very attractive to one of today's bright young scientists, who would probably work harder when he has a chance to get rich as a result. In the not-too-distant past, though, entrepreneurship was the exception among researchers. Bright young scientists generally remained content to enjoy the safety of a "good job" in a solid corporation. Patents added to one's prestige and job security, but the employer kept the lion's share of their value. Today, however, it is a quantum leap easier for a bright researcher to convert an idea into the seed for a new company. Lured by the prospect of riches and prodded by the prospect of failure, the modern entrepreneur is exposed to far stronger incentives than was his "company-man" father and thus is potentially more productive.

Large corporations that cannot keep their brightest researchers happy within the salary structures of hierarchical organizations must find ways to cooperate with startups. Du Pont and Monsanto, for example, have both learned the advantages of letting young, small organizations conduct research and then stepping on stage themselves when products are ready for manufacturing and marketing. Du Pont has recently been buying up new companies that have developed biotechnology products in agrichemicals and pharmaceuticals, areas in which its own research efforts have come up short. Du Pont is also trying joint ventures, which it traditionally shunned in order to keep its research efforts confidential.[15] Monsanto, too, is sampling the benefits of cooperation with new ventures. In a recent interview CEO Richard J. Mahoney stated, "Monsanto decided it wanted to be in the biotechnology and pharmaceutical business many years ago. . . . In fact, we were helping start up a number of these companies with venture capital. We bought Continental Pharmaceutical last year because we had a number of leads that had to be developed, and we didn't have anybody to develop them."[16] Lacking the necessary in-house capability, Chrysler, as well, has turned to a joint venture—in this case with a Silicon Valley artificial intelligence startup to bring expert systems into Chrysler cars in the '90s.

Du Pont, Monsanto, and Chrysler are not alone in seeking outside help for new product development. Indeed, one of Silicon Valley's latest contributions to the lexicon of business is the "wizard shop."[17] Schlage Lock Company, the leading maker of mechanical locks, for example, turned to San Francisco's Theta Resources for the design work on an electronic lock system for hotels. Schlage's own internal R&D efforts had come up dry after a five-year effort. Theta Resources completed the job in just 18 months, and Schlage now has two patents plus a backlog of orders for its system.

Theta Resources is not alone, and the list of customers contains some surprises. David Kelley Design of Palo Alto, for example, designed the mouse that is so familiar to users of the Macintosh computer. Stephen Beck and Edward Goldfarb of Beck-Tech designed the innards of an electronic hand puppet, Talking Wrinkles, for Coleco Industries' 1986 Christmas toy line. Burt Rutan, himself a "wizard" in aviation circles (his Mojave, California, firm builds exotic flying prototypes for aerospace firms, such as Raytheon's Beech Aircraft Division), turned to Robert Conn's Connsult Inc. to design a microelectronic monitor to continuously record the airspeed and altitude of the Voyager on its historic round-the-world flight.

Finally, SRI International, a contract-research laboratory head-quartered in Menlo Park, California, may be on its way to becoming the granddaddy of all wizard shops. General Electric recently gave its Sarnoff Laboratory to SRI. The Sarnoff Lab, which developed color television, the liquid crystal display, and the VCR, to name a few of its achievements, came to GE in the latter's merger with RCA. Sarnoff's New Jersey facilities give SRI a strong presence on both coasts and make it a formidable factor in research circles.[18] The increasing opportunities in the financial markets for young, vigorous technology startup compa-nies spell an erosion of competitive advantage in R&D for large, integrated corporations, while stimulating the development of new technologies.

SUMMARY

The financial marketplace is maturing rapidly, well on its way to attaining a truly worldwide scope, and the array of opportuni-ties offered to investors is proliferating at a breakneck pace. The optimist sees opportunity in this, and indeed, the opportunities for people with good ideas have never in all of history been greater. Nor have the opportunities for those with cash ever been greater. When a mature corporation in a dead-end industry, however, disgorges its cash, there may be different interpreta-tions. Some observers see the "invisible hand" at work, perceiv-ing that it leads to results that may never have been intended but that raise the productivity of society as a whole. Others, however, may see only the lifeblood draining from an established, vener-able institution.

So long as vigorous new enterprises are nourished in the process, though, we are all better off. Perhaps the hardest aspect for many to accept is that decisions that once were indisputably in the province of conscious decision making by an elite corps of minds are increasingly being made in the faceless, apparently chaotic marketplace—but in the end comes the realization that this is indeed a step toward greater democracy in economic affairs.

NOTES

1. Edwin Cannan, ed., *The Wealth of Nations*, p. 477.

2. A similar play on words was used recently in another context by Brock and Magee, "The Invisible Foot."

3. Spence, "The Economics of Internal Organization," pp. 163–72.

4. The implications of a departure from the "mini capital market" syndrome are explored in John Martin and John Kensinger, "Royalty Trusts, Master Partnerships, and Other Organizational Means of 'Unfirming' the Firm," pp. 72–80.

5. R. H. Coase, "The Nature of the Firm," pp. 386–405.

6. See H. Leland and D. Pyle, "Informational Asymmetries," pp. 371–87. This agency cost problem is referred to as the "cost of informational asymmetry." Although it might arise with any external financing, it tends to be higher for equity than for debt.

7. Bradford Cornell and Alan Shapiro, "Corporate Stakeholders," pp.5–14.

8. As did Exxon, Mobil, and Sohio, much to their chagrin.

9. John J. McConnell and Chris J. Muscarella, "Corporate Capital Expenditure Decisions," pp. 399–422.

10. For a complete analysis of the benefits, see Andrew Chen and John Kensinger, pp. 44–51.

11. For a review of project financing for R&D and a discussion of its contribution to the set of organizational possibilities, see John Kensinger and John Martin, "Project Financing for Research and Development," pp. 119–148.

12. For more on the regulatory dialectic, see Andrew Chen and John Kensinger, pp. 44–51. See also E. Kane, "Good Intentions and Unintended Evil," pp. 55–69.

13. Ian Cooper and Julian Franks, "Treasury Performance Measurement," pp. 29–43.

14. For a detailed analysis of the Exxon transaction, see John D. Finnerty, "Zero Coupon Bond Arbitrage," pp. 13–17.

15. See C. S. Eklund and J. L. Cowan, "What's Causing the Scratches," pp. 60f.

16. "Richard J. Mahoney Reshapes Monsanto for the Future," pp. 1–3.

17. See Michael Rogers, "Silicon Valley's Newest Wizards," pp. 36–37.

18. See Otis Port, Evert Clark, and James Norman, "GE Gift-Wraps a Landmark Lab," p. 35.

REFERENCES

Brock, William A., and Stephen P. Magee. "The Invisible Foot and the Waste of Nations: Redistribution and Economic Growth," in David

C. Colander, ed., *Neoclassical Political Economy* (Boston, MA: Ballinger, 1984).

Cannan, Edwin, ed., *The Wealth of Nations*, Vol. 1 (Chicago: The University of Chicago Press, 1976).

Chen, Andrew, and John Kensinger. "Innovations in Corporate Financing: Tax-Deductible Equity," *Financial Management* 15 (Winter 1985), pp. 44–51.

Coase, R. H. "The Nature of the Firm," *Econometrica* (November 1937), pp. 386–405.

Cooper, Ian, and Julian Franks. "Treasury Performance Measurement," *Midland Corporate Finance Journal* 4 (Winter 1987), pp. 29–43.

Cornell, Bradford, and Alan Shapiro. "Corporate Stakeholders and Corporate Finance," *Financial Management* 16 (Spring 1987), pp. 5–14.

Eklund, C. S., and A. L. Cowan. "What's Causing the Scratches in DuPont's Teflon," *Business Week* (December 8, 1986), pp. 60f.

Finnerty, John D. "Zero Coupon Bond Arbitrage: An Illustration of the Regulatory Dialectic at Work," *Financial Management* 14 (Winter 1985), pp. 13–17.

Jensen, Michael C. "Agency Costs of Free Cash Flow, Corporate Finance and Takeovers," *American Economic Review* (May 1986), pp. 323–29.

Kane, E. "Good Intentions and Unintended Evil: The Case Against Selective Credit Allocation," *Journal of Money, Credit, and Banking* (February 1977), pp. 55–69.

Leland, H., and D. Pyle. "Informational Asymmetries, Financial Structure, and Financial Intermediation," *Journal of Finance* 32 (May 1977), pp. 371–87.

Kensinger, John, and John Martin. "Royalty Trusts, Master Partnerships, and Other Organizational Means of 'Unfirming' the Firm," *Midland Corporate Finance Journal* 4 (Summer 1986), pp. 72–80. Reprinted in Stern, Stewart, and Chew (eds.), *Corporate Restructuring and Executive Compensation* (Cambridge, MA: Ballinger, 1989).

Kensinger, John, and John Martin. "Project Financing for Research and Development," *Research in Finance*, Vol. 8 (1990), pp. 119–48.

Martin, John, and John Kensinger. "An Economic Analysis of R&D Limited Partnerships," *Midland Corporate Finance Journal* 3 (Winter 1986), pp. 33–45. Reprinted in Stern, Stewart, and Chew (eds.), *Corporate Restructuring and Executive Compensation* (Cambridge, MA: Ballinger, 1989).

McConnell, John J., and Chris J. Muscarella. "Corporate Capital Expenditure Decisions and the Market Value of the Firm," *Journal of Financial Economics* (September 1985), pp. 399–422.

Port, Otis, Evert Clark, and James Norman. "GE Gift-Wraps a Landmark Lab," *Business Week* (February 16, 1987), p. 35.

"Richard J. Mahoney Reshapes Monsanto for the Future," *DH&S Review*, Deloitte Haskins & Sells (December 9, 1985), pp. 1-3.

Rogers, Michael. "Silicon Valley's Newest Wizards," *Newsweek* (January 5, 1987), pp. 36-37.

Spence, A. M. "The Economics of Internal Organization: An Introduction," *Bell Journal of Economics* (Spring 1975), pp. 163-72.

Government Documents

Tax Reform Act of 1984
Tax Reform Act of 1986
Tax Act of 1987

Chapter 3

Equity with a Money-Back Guarantee

One of the financial innovations that investment bankers have come up with recently is a common stock that can be "put" back to the issuer. A "puttable stock" can be used to reduce the underpricing problem in some initial public offerings as well as to resolve other problems arising from informational asymmetry. Although puttable stock is classified as equity on the issuing corporation's financial statements, from the investor's point of view it is comparable to a convertible bond. Thus it has attractive features for a corporation that would like to sell convertible bonds but needs a financing arrangement that can be treated as equity for accounting and other purposes.

Tax considerations don't adequately explain the invention of this hybrid security. For corporations that have an existing equity base and an established taxable income stream, in fact, convertible bonds, especially the zero-coupon variety, are preferable. The corporation issuing zero-coupon convertibles incurs no cash outlay before the maturity date but gets a tax deduction for "interest" as it accrues. The holder foregoes cash payment of accrued interest in the event the conversion option is exercised. We conclude, however, that informational asymmetry and other market imperfections explain the advent of puttable stock. It has the potential to be a useful tool for initial public offerings, for external financing for companies with relatively high degrees of leverage, or for contingencies that require the sale of equity when management believes that the stock is undervalued by the market.

To meet SEC requirements for treatment as an equity financing, the issuer of puttable stock must be able to meet its obligations under the guarantee by issuing more shares of common stock. Other options may also be available to the issuer, so that the puts may be paid off in cash, notes (with predefined face value, maturity, and floating interest rates), or preferred stock. One of these optional settlement methods would be optimal if the rights were presented for payment at a time when management believes that the common stock is undervalued by the market. These optional settlement methods also provide an efficient means of out-of-court settlement in event of the puttable stock equivalent of bankruptcy, when the total market value of equity in the firm is less than the amount of the guarantee. Thus, when the issuer has the option to make the payoff on the puts in cash, notes, or other senior securities, issuing puttable stock may offer additional advantages over convertible debt.

EXAMPLES OF COMMON STOCK THAT CAN BE "PUT" BACK TO THE ISSUER

Puttable stock was invented by Drexel Burnham Lambert, an investment banking firm, in a development process involving two separate clients. The first step occurred in November 1984, when Drexel designed a financing package for the $6 million initial public offering of stock for Arley Merchandise Corporation. Each unit consisted of a share of common stock with a "right" providing the option to sell the stock back to the company for cash or notes.[1] The Arley units were offered at $8 each, with accompanying rights for investors to "put" their stock back to the company for $8 per share two years later.[2] These were European-type puts, which could not be exercised early.

The Securities and Exchange Commission (SEC), however, subsequently ruled that a package like Arley's must be treated as redeemable equity and placed on the company's books as debt until the puts expired. Soon afterwards, Drexel applied this experience to find an innovative solution for the problem of another client. Drexel not only succeeded in satisfying the regulators but also demonstrated that puttable stock can be used in other situations besides initial public offerings.

Another company, Gearhart Industries (an oil- and gas-drilling services company) needed to raise a large amount of money under a short deadline. After a long and sometimes bitter struggle in which Smith International, Inc., tried to take over Gearhart, an agreement was reached in March 1985 for Gearhart to buy back 5.3 million shares of its stock from Smith at $15 per share (a total of about $80 million). Unfortunately, the market price of Gearhart's stock was fluctuating around $10.75 per share.[3] Unable to raise the necessary cash by means of an issue of new preferred stock or debt in time to meet the deadline, but concerned about selling common stock at a time when the price was at a record low, Gearhart turned to Drexel for help. Drexel arranged a public offering of common stock as part of a puttable stock package, with each share protected by a Gearhart-issued put.[4]

In order to avoid the difficulties created by the SEC ruling on the Arley case, Gearhart's puttable stock was made redeemable in cash, debt, preferred stock, or common stock, at the option of the issuer.[5] This modification overcame the regulatory hurdle. Because the arrangement allowed Gearhart the option of issuing common stock to meet its obligation under the guarantee, the SEC ruled that this was a bona fide equity financing. The puttable stock issue was sold in "units," each of which consisted of five shares of common stock and five rights to sell those shares back to Gearhart for a guaranteed price.[6]

The favorable SEC ruling creates a potential cost for the existing shareholders who, in effect, write the puts. If the puts were redeemed by issuing more shares of common stock, owners of the puttable stock units would receive enough extra shares to bring the value of their units back up to the guaranteed amount. By opting to meet the guarantee with additional common stock, the issuer fulfills its obligations by transferring a larger share of ownership to the protected shareholder group, at the expense of the original shareholders. If the issuer should experience particularly hard times and the total market value of all outstanding equity falls below the guaranteed floor value of the puttable stock issue, the steps taken to satisfy the guarantee would result in a substantial transfer of ownership of the corporation to the holders of the puttable stock. The founders and earlier stockholders of the company could be left with very little.

In effect, then, the steps taken to satisfy the guarantee are analogous to bankruptcy. There are legal limits to the issuer's ability to meet the guarantee by issuing more shares, however, necessitating a supplementary mechanism for going "bankrupt" (otherwise, the proceeds from the sale of puttable stock would suffer because the guarantee would lack integrity). Such a mechanism is provided when multiple payoff options are available to the issuer, allowing the puts to be paid off with cash, notes, or a special class of preferred stock.

Despite the potential problems created by the issuance of the puts, the market price of Gearhart stock showed no significant reaction to the announcement, suggesting that the terms were perceived as fair. On the announcement date (March 28, 1985) Gearhart stock gained 12.5 cents (up 2.4 percent) while the S&P 500 index held steady. This one-tick gain was well within the normal range of fluctuation for Gearhart. Over the five trading days surrounding the announcement (March 26 to April 1) the average daily residual was a mere 0.12 percent.[7] Over the period March 4 to May 3, 1985 (18 trading days prior to the announcement and 25 after) the average daily market-adjusted residual was near zero (-.001) with standard deviation of 2.05 percent. The biggest single-day gain over the interval was 4.98 percent on April 25, and the biggest loss was 5.92 percent on March 12. The cumulative residual averaged -1.85 percent over this period (with standard deviation of 3.16 percent), and ended the period at 0.6 percent.

A COMPARISON WITH CONVERTIBLE DEBT

Drexel argues that since listed puts are not available to provide protection for IPO investors, the puttable stock innovation provides an attractive investment opportunity that is not otherwise available.[8] Holding the puttable stock is not, however, the same as holding the stock and a put together in a portfolio. One difference is that the right conveyed in a puttable stock unit is a European-type option that cannot be exercised prior to expiration, while listed puts are American options that can be exercised any time prior to expiration. With puttable stock, furthermore, the puts are written by one group of the company's stockholders (referred to here as the founders) and issued to another group of stockholders, thus creating two distinct stockholder groups. If the puts are exercised, the result will be a transfer of ownership claims from one group to the other.

The key to the valuation of a puttable stock lies in the payoffs to be received by the holders in different states of the world (defined in terms of the total market value of the issuing firm). To lay a foundation for understanding the nature of a puttable stock, we analyze the payoffs to three investment alternatives: a puttable stock, a convertible bond, and a portfolio containing a common stock and an ordinary protective put.[9] The analysis focuses on the situation of a corporation making its initial public offering and demonstrates that in a frictionless environment the payoffs are identical for holders of a puttable stock and for holders of zero-coupon convertible bonds, showing that Ingersoll's model is applicable to puttable stock as well as convertible bonds.[10]

Exhibit 1 lists the definitions of symbols. The simplifying assumptions are listed below, in the order in which they will later be relaxed.

1. The issuing firm starts with a clean slate, having no outstanding debt. All past financing has come from equity investments by the founders. The corporation pays no dividends and intends to continue this policy until maturity of the puts.

Exhibit 1
Definitions of Symbols

List of Symbols

n	=	number of shares retained by the founders
N	=	number of shares sold to the public
α	=	$N/(N+n)$ = proportion of firm offered to public
S	=	guaranteed value per share
G	=	NS = total amount of guaranteed payment
S'	=	market value per share on exercise date, ex-rights
V'	=	$(N+n)S'$ = value of the firm on exercise date
V	=	current market value of the firm
m	=	number of shares transferred under the guarantee
t	=	time remaining until exercise date

2. Information is fully and costlessly available to all participants in the marketplace.

3. The put provision is conveyed by rights that can be exercised only on the expiration date. The guarantee will be honored by transferring additional common stock to the holders of puts, and the capital market fully anticipates the dilution effects of such an issue of additional common stock. The number of additional shares will be determined on the basis of the market value. For example, if the guaranteed floor is $15 per unit and the market price of the stock has dropped to $10 per share, an investor holding 100 puttable stock units would receive an extra 50 shares.[11]

4. The guarantee will be fully honored, with adjustments to protect the holders of puttable stock from dilution. One means of doing so would be for the founders to give

up some of their own shares in order to meet the
guarantee, so that no new shares would be issued (other
adjustment procedures are available that would accomplish the same effect).

5. In the analysis, convertible bonds are compared to the
puttable common stock. Each of the bonds is convertible
at the end of the period into one share of common stock.
N units are sold. The face value of each unit of debt is
S, and the total face value of the issue is NS. The holders
may take the face value or opt for stock. In event of
default on the bonds, bankruptcy is costless.

6. The choice of puttable stock or convertible bonds has no
impact on the corporation's ability to carry out its
business activities—that is, the financing choice does not
affect important qualities such as relationships with
customers or suppliers.

Exhibit 2 summarizes the payoffs from each alternative on the
expiration date. If the terminal share value were less than the
guaranteed price (that is, S' < S), we need to differentiate two
separate sets of outcomes that could occur:

1. The value of the firm is less than the total guaranteed
payment, so the firm will not be able to fully meet the
guarantee, even if the founders give up their entire stake.
This condition is expressed by V' < G.

2. The value of the firm is equal to or greater than the total
amount of the guarantee, so the guarantee could be met
while leaving the founders with something to spare. This
condition is expressed as G < V' < (N+n)S:

In both of these two cases, holders of stock plus an ordinary
put would exercise their puts, and in aggregate would receive G,
the guaranteed payment. However, if V' < G, holders of puttable
stock would receive no more than the value of the firm. The same

Exhibit 2
Payoffs at Expiration

	Firm Value at Expiration		
Strategy:	V' < G	G < V' < (N+n)S	(N+n)S < V'
Stock plus Put	G	G	NS' = αV'
Puttable Stock	V'	(N+m)S' = G	NS' = αV'
Convertible Debt	V'	NS = G	NS' = αV'

is true of holders of convertible bonds, because the issuer would default its bond obligations and leave the bondholders with the entire firm.

If the terminal value of a share of stock exceeded the guaranteed price (that is, $S' > S$) holders of stock plus puts would throw away their puts, because they expire out of the money. If such investors held a total of N shares, they would hold securities with an aggregate value of NS', and would own an α share of the firm. Another way of expressing the condition in this case is to say that the market value of the firm, V', equals or exceeds the product of the guaranteed price multiplied by the total number of shares outstanding, $(N+n)S$ (this is the way the condition is shown in Exhibit 2). Holders of puttable stock would enjoy the same aggregate value in this case, as they would not exercise their puts. Holders of convertible debt would convert in this case, and their aggregate holding would also be NS'.

Thus it can be seen that the payoffs from holding puttable stock are not in all cases the same as the payoffs from holding a portfolio of stock plus the ordinary puts. The payoff from holding puttable stock is, however, the same in all cases as the payoff from holding convertible bonds. Exhibit 3 shows graphically the terminal value of the public holding of either puttable stock or convertible bonds, in relation to the total value of the issuing firm.

Exhibit 3
Value of Puttable Stock or Convertible Bonds at Maturity

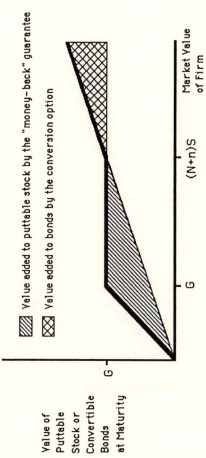

Value of
Puttable
Stock or
Convertible
Bonds
at Maturity

G

☒ Value added to puttable stock by the "money-back" guarantee
☒ Value added to bonds by the conversion option

G   (N+n)S   Market Value
of Firm

The owners of puttable stock collectively own a portfolio consisting of an α share of the firm and two put options. One is a long put option to sell an α fraction of the firm for the guaranteed amount. The other is a short put, which represents an obligation to accept the *whole* firm in place of the guaranteed amount (the issuers of the guarantee retain the right to make good on it by turning over the whole firm, even if it is worth less than the amount of the guarantee). By applying the put-call parity relationship, it can be shown that puttable stock fits Ingersoll's valuation model for zero-coupon convertible bonds.[12] Prior to expiration, the current market value of the firm (V) is of course the upper bound for the value of puttable stock or convertible bonds. The lower bound is αV, and the value of puttable stock or convertible bonds prior to expiration must fall between these bounds. The function is expressed graphically in Exhibit 4. (The simplified version of Ingersoll's valuation model of zero-coupon convertible bonds is described in an appendix to this chapter.)

The mechanics of exercising the options in a puttable stock package are different from a convertible bond package, so there may be differences in transaction costs that do not show up in Exhibit 4. More complex differences arise when a comparison is made between puttable stock and coupon-paying convertible bonds. Holders of puttable stock receive any dividends declared, but there are no specific promises as there are in the case of coupon payments for bonds. Failure to pay a coupon, of course, could precipitate bankruptcy. Issuing puttable stock does not carry the same risk, therefore, as issuing coupon-paying convertible bonds.

It should be noted that the estimate of the variance rate of the company's market value is one of the key factors in the application of the Black-Scholes option pricing model (OPM) to evaluate puttable stock. For an issuing firm that has a stock price history, the estimation of the variance rate of the company's value can be accomplished by using the historical data of its stock prices. On the other hand, if the puttable stock is an IPO situation, one must rely on other measures (such as cash flows of the firm or the price

Exhibit 4
Value of Puttable Stock or Convertible Bonds Prior to Maturity

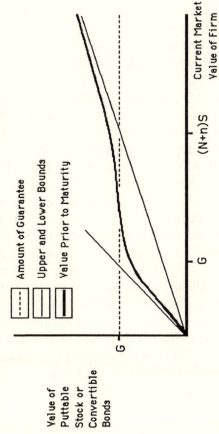

Value of Puttable Stock or Convertible Bonds

Amount of Guarantee
Upper and Lower Bounds
Value Prior to Maturity

G

G   (N+n)S   Current Market Value of Firm

history of a comparable company) to estimate the variance rate for the purpose of pricing the puttable stock.

In the foregoing analysis we assume away dividends and bankruptcy resulting from prior borrowings (refer to assumption 1). Thus the European/American dichotomy that distinguishes puttable stock from convertible bonds does not matter. This dichotomy, however, deserves further attention. Even though a convertible bond may be exercised prior to maturity, this privilege does not necessarily make it more valuable than an otherwise identical puttable stock. The holders of puttable stock also have seniority over unprotected stockholders in the event bankruptcy is declared prior to the maturity of the puts. Therefore, early exercise in the event of bankruptcy is, in effect, provided for. Because an option is generally worth more alive than dead while the underlying asset is still viable, the rational reason for early exercise of a convertible bond is to receive the dividends if the company begins making cash distributions to stockholders. Although the option in a puttable stock unit cannot be exercised early, the holder already possesses the stock and therefore automatically receives any dividends that might be declared.

Even so, there is a possibility for a wealth transfer from the puttable stockholders to the founding shareholders under extreme circumstances. Consider a situation in which the company experiences severe difficulties and the probability becomes substantial that the value of the company will be less than enough to meet the guarantee. The reasonable expectation in such a circumstance is that the equivalent of bankruptcy will occur, and ownership of the company will shift substantially to the holders of puttable stock (with the founding shareholders being left only a remnant). Because the puts cannot be exercised early, the founding shareholders have an opportunity (while they are still in control) to declare dividends, in order to receive a portion of the wealth that would otherwise revert to the protected stockholders upon maturity of the puts. A restriction on distributions to shareholders under such circumstances is needed, therefore, to protect the integrity of the guarantee and reduce the cost of capital for the puttable stock issue. In the Gearhart case such restrictions existed in prior covenants. With the proper protection against welshing, the European nature of the option in puttable stock units creates no disadvantage for the holder.

ADVANTAGES OF GIVING A MONEY-BACK GUARANTEE

In the previous section puttable stock is shown to be equivalent to convertible bonds under a certain set of assumptions. Relaxing some of the assumptions reveals several advantages puttable stock has over convertible bonds.

Reduced Informational Asymmetry Costs

In an IPO, the founders of the firm are fundamentally interested in minimizing the share of ownership they must relinquish in order to obtain the financial resources necessary to realize their firm's potential. When the founders are better informed about the prospects of the firm than are outside investors, they chafe at the prospect of selling what they consider to be undervalued equity claims but assign a low probability to the prospect that the guarantee in a puttable stock issue would be exercised. In that case there would be informational asymmetry costs associated with the sale of new "plain vanilla" common stock.

Leland and Pyle first described informational asymmetry costs. The problem can arise with any form of external financing, and its essence can be explained fairly simply. Managers often possess valuable information about new projects that cannot be unambiguously communicated to the capital market. One potential barrier to communication is the need to keep competitors in the dark in order to maintain the competitive advantage that makes the project potentially profitable. Whenever such an informational asymmetry exists, managers face a problem. If new claims against the firm are sold in the capital market, they will be undervalued due to the lack of complete information. That is, their market value will be less than their fair value, and the difference constitutes a type of agency cost. Different forms of financing produce different informational asymmetry costs, and the costs are higher for equity than debt. It is management's job to find ways to finance new projects that minimize the informational asymmetry costs borne by existing shareholders.

By using the equivalent of convertible debt to gain the funds it needs, a company can reduce the informational asymmetry cost. The willingness to put existing shareholders on the line in order to protect new shareholders from loss not only reduces the risk faced by the new shareholders but may also serve as a means of signaling to them the implications of the information held by the insiders. Such signaling could enhance the value of the new issue even beyond what would be justified by the risk reduction alone. Moreover, by packaging the financing as puttable stock, the issuing firm is able at the same time to preserve the advantages of equity.

In his recent empirical study of the cost of going public, Ritter concluded that explicit and implicit costs can absorb 30 percent or more of the proceeds in the case of a small initial public offering (compared to an average of 21 percent for firm commitment IPOs of all sizes). Ritter identifies informational asymmetry as a significant contributing factor in such high costs, drawing upon earlier work by Rock and Beatty and Ritter. In initial public offerings, informed investors will submit more purchase orders for underpriced offers than for overpriced offers, with the result that uninformed investors (who wind up with the residual) will receive a relatively larger portion of shares in overpriced offers and a relatively smaller portion of shares in underpriced offers. Over several offers, therefore, the uninformed investors can expect to receive more than their fair share of dogs and less than their fair share of good deals (thus they are afflicted by the "winners' curse" familiar to those who often bid too high at auctions and so tend to overpay). Ritter describes the condition of the uninformed investors by saying that their expected return conditional on receiving shares is lower than their expected return conditional on submitting a purchase order. To fully subscribe an issue when a large proportion of investors consider themselves to be uninformed therefore requires a greater degree of underpricing than would be the case if ignorance were less widespread.

A best-efforts offering is one way to resolve the problem. The adverse selection problem that confronts the uninformed investors in a firm commitment is reduced in a best-efforts offering, since the offer will be withdrawn if it is not fully subscribed. The risk that is born by uninformed investors in a firm commitment is shifted to the issuer in a best-efforts offering. Thus the majority of small initial public offerings (less than $4 million proceeds) are best-efforts offerings. A major concern for the issuers is that the offer may be withdrawn, however, leaving them without the necessary capital.

Puttable stock is another alternative which could significantly reduce the costs to uninformed investors (lifting the pall cast over them by the winners' curse) and thus be particularly helpful in facilitating access to public equity capital by small startup companies. Offering the protection of the puts would provide a way of reducing the underpricing required by uninformed investors in a firm commitment. Through the puts, the risk to the uninformed investors would be shifted to the founding shareholders of the issuing corporation, and the corporation could be assured of raising the necessary capital.

The motivation for trying puttable stock in the first place was that the owners of Arley Merchandise Corporation were unwilling to accept less than $8 per share, but Drexel believed the stock would fetch only about $6 in the market. Making the stock puttable enabled the package to be offered at $8 per unit, with the accompanying rights (the official term for the puts) permitting investors to sell their stock back to the company at $8 per share two years later (these were European puts, which could not be exercised early). The stock and rights could be separated and traded independently, however, at the discretion of the holder.

The rights were listed on the Boston Stock Exchange. The Arley common stock (sans rights) began trading on the American

Stock Exchange on November 15, 1984, closing at $7.625 per share, and the "seasoning" of Arley stock took a decidedly different course than the average IPO. Rather than rising substantially in the early rounds of public trading—the fate of the typical underpriced fledgling stock—Arley settled quickly to the $6 level predicted by Drexel. Exhibit 5 shows the market-adjusted cumulative residuals for Arley over the first three months of trading.[13] Over the first four full weeks of trading the cumulative residual dropped off precipitously, falling to –25.65 percent at the close of December 12. During this time, the average daily residual was –0.35 percent (with a standard deviation of 1.37 percent). After this adjustment period, Arley fluctuated randomly (albeit noisily) around $6 per share until it began a steady climb in April 1986. The cumulative market-adjusted residual averaged –18.16 percent (with standard deviation of 5.87%) over the 137 trading days from December 13, 1984 to June 28, 1985. The individual daily residuals averaged nearly zero (.000026) over this post-adjustment period, however, with standard deviation of 3.27 percent.

The willingness of Arley's original owners to shoulder the downside risk for new stockholders allowed Arley to collect a $2 premium over the $6 market value of its stock. This single experiment does not provide a prudent basis to say that puttable stock can do the same on average over a large number of IPOs, but it does provide an incentive for further experimentation.

A postscript is in order, to complete the Arley story. On August 18, 1986, the directors accepted an offer from a group of middle managers to buy Arley for $48.7 million, with public stockholders scheduled to receive $10 cash per share. Pending the close of this sale, the stock was trading in the range of $9 to $10 during the exercise period of the puts, so they expired unused.

The discussion up to this point has been concerned with informational asymmetry that exists at the time of the issue. Informational asymmetry costs could also arise at the time the puts mature, and can be reduced by the alternative settlement methods (the option to pay off the put-holders in cash, notes, or preferred stock). Suppose that when the puts mature, manage-

Exhibit 5
Arley Cumulative Residuals

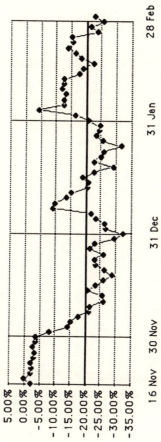

ment has reason to believe that the market value of the corporation is depressed because important information is not available in the marketplace. Paying off the put-holders with undervalued common stock would not be in the best interests of the original (unprotected) shareholders. A payoff in cash, notes, or redeemable preferred stock would then be more advantageous.

More Efficient Mechanisms for Handling Default

For purposes of gaining a favorable SEC ruling on the treatment of a puttable stock as equity, it is sufficient if common stock is the only option available to the issuer for meeting the obligations to holders of puts. Additional options, including cash, notes, or preferred stock, are necessary in order to provide a means of effecting the puttable stock equivalent of bankruptcy (which occurs when the resources of the corporation are insufficient to meet the obligations created by the guarantee). Due to the legal restrictions on the maximum number of shares a corporation can issue under its charter, such alternatives are required in order to make the puts fully credible to potential investors. If the market value of the issuing corporation falls below the guaranteed amount, that is, a mechanism is needed to effect the transfer of ownership to the holders of puttable stock.

A good example is provided by the preferred stock alternative in the Gearhart case, which was described in detail in the prospectus for the puttable stock issue. Any new preferred stock issued to satisfy the guarantee would have the same par value and pay the same dividend as common stock, would convey full voting rights, and would convey a prior claim in event of bankruptcy. If the preferred stock alternative were offered, holders of puttable stock would have the opportunity to exchange their shares of common stock for an appropriate number of shares of preferred stock.[14] The original stockholders can default on the guarantee and the lion's share of the company can be transferred to the puttable stockholders without imposing the delays and expense of filing for bankruptcy. Moreover, the process of transferring control is an automatic consequence that follows from fulfilling the contractual obligations imposed by the puttable stock agreement.

One of the advantages of puttable stock over convertible bonds, therefore, is the relative efficiency with which the transfer of ownership takes place in the event of default. This greater efficiency should be reflected in a higher price paid for puttable stock (relative to convertible bonds) at the time of issue, and hence a lower cost of capital for puttable stock.

As an illustration, consider the example of a corporation with 500,000 shares outstanding (held, say, by the founders) that issues an additional 500,000 shares of puttable stock with a guaranteed floor value of $50 million. The market value of the corporation was $100 million ($100 per share) at the time of the issue. The corporate charter, furthermore, limits the total number of shares the firm can issue to 4 million.

Suppose that catastrophe strikes, and the value of the corporation drops. The market would anticipate dilution as the expiration of the puts approaches, and the decline in per share values would accelerate. If the corporation lost 40 percent of its value and were worth $60 million at the time the puts expired, for example, the holders of puttable stock as a group would receive enough new shares so that they would own 5 out of every 6 shares outstanding. Since the founding shareholders own 500,000 shares, the total number of outstanding shares would have to increase to 3 million, and the price per share would drop to $20 (an 80 percent decline). The total value of the founding shareholders' position would be $10 million, while the 2.5 million shares in the hands of the protected stockholders would have a total value of $50 million. Thus, all of the decline would be borne by the founding shareholder group, which is consistent with the spirit of the guarantee.[15]

If the market value of the corporation dropped to $55 million, however, the total number of shares would have to be increased to 5.5 million ($10 per share) in order to meet the guarantee; but this number exceeds the legal limitation imposed by the corporate charter. Therefore an alternative means of payment is necessary in order to maintain the integrity of the guarantee.

Meeting the obligation with cash would require a substantial liquidation of the company. Paying with notes would create the prospect of bankruptcy at a future date. Thus, either option would result in the realignment of ownership required to make good on the guarantee. The firm might be worth more as a going concern than in liquidation, however, making a cash settlement unattractive. The prospect of costly bankruptcy proceedings, furthermore, could cause the notes to be considered inefficient. In such cases, the option of satisfying the guarantee by offering preferred shares provides the necessary integrity.

Improved Relationships with Customers and Suppliers

Puttable stock should be considered a worthwhile innovation only if it provides benefits that are not available with convertible debt.[16] The final assumption to be relaxed is that there is no interrelation between the financing decisions of the firm and its value. In the case of a mature corporation, there are many tax considerations, agency problems, and control issues that may make capital structure relevant, and these issues are already familiar to the reader. For the young firm just starting out, tax considerations do not become relevant until a taxable earnings stream has been established. In such a case there are other considerations that may dictate the choice of a financing arrangement that is widely acknowledged to be equity (even if it is a hybrid). Convertible debt would not suffice in such a situation, but puttable common stock would be satisfactory.

Alan Shapiro recently provided evidence that the net present value a firm is able to generate derives in substantial part from its ability to maintain a competitive advantage. Potential customers may evaluate a prospective purchase on the basis of the producer's financial strength as well as the average quality of its products. People are often leery of buying from a company that may not survive to give future product support to those customers who get the occasional lemon. Likewise, a firm that projects the appearance of financial strength may enjoy more advantageous relationships with suppliers of everything from loans to labor to nuts and bolts.

Horowitz and Kolodny found evidence of this in a study of the impact of new accounting rules on the level of R&D expenditure by firms.[17] Many of the firms that were forced to switch to immediate expensing of R&D, particularly smaller companies, subsequently reduced their commitment to R&D. Horowitz and Kolodny concluded that this action, although it hurt the companies' long-term competitive position, was taken in order to avert even more serious near-term harm that might arise purely from accounting effects. Some of the highlights of their list of concerns were:

1. Listing requirements of the various stock exchanges include a minimum reported earnings requirement.

2. Federal government regulations concerning the determination of a firm's acceptability as a government contractor include a number of accounting ratios that must be within acceptable ranges.

3. Banks and other institutional lenders may also place undue emphasis on accounting numbers as opposed to the economic reality of the firm's financial condition.

For similar reasons a firm, particularly a smaller one, may find that equity financing is the only viable way to raise needed capital while preserving the accounting data necessary to allow it to have its stock listed, gain federal contracts, and enjoy good relations with banks and other financial institutions.

Reduced Agency Costs

Even for a corporation that is well beyond the IPO stage, puttable stock may provide a solution for agency problems in special circumstances. General Motors, for example, recently issued an "E Class" common stock whose dividends are pegged to the performance of the Electronic Data Systems (EDS) division (they later issued an "H Class" common stock with dividends pegged to the performance of the Hughes Aircraft division). These new classes of common stock create a company within a company. The separate parts have different owners who receive differential rewards, although the whole is controlled by a single management. When these different groups have conflicting interests, complex agency problems arise.

The creation of the E Class stock, for instance, has given rise to controversies over transfer pricing for goods and services supplied to other divisions by EDS. High transfer prices are in the best interests of the owners of E Class stock (many of whom are key employees of the EDS division), but hurt the performance of the remainder of the corporation. Likewise, artificially low transfer prices for services supplied by the EDS division would hurt the owners of E Class stock. Given uncertainty over how upper management will resolve transfer pricing difficulties in the future, the market values of all classes of stock suffer. Owners of E Class stock have cause to be concerned that upper management may enhance the value of the regular stock at the expense of E Class stock. At the same time, owners of regular stock may worry that upper management will grant concessions to EDS in order to provide enhanced incentives to key employees of that division.

If a special class of stock were puttable to the parent corporation, however, the owners would be assured of redress in the event of a series of adverse decisions by upper management. Investors would therefore be willing to pay a higher price for the special class of stock, and upper management would have an incentive to make better-balanced decisions.

Toward a Better Put

An obvious concern with the Arley and Gearhart puts was that they were backed only by the company issuing the puttable stock.

This feature in turn leads to the equivalence with convertible debt. An obvious improvement therefore is to provide stronger support for the money-back guarantee. This was done in the case of a commodity-trading partnership formed in 1988. Limited partnership units in the Dean Witter Principal Guaranteed Fund L. P. were sold for $1,000 each, with a money-back guarantee at the end of five years. These put options were issued by a special-purpose "guarantee corporation," which gained its substance from an irrevocable letter of credit issued by Citicorp bank.

Of course, Citibank collected an explicit fee for this service. Furthermore, the contract with Citibank provides explicit criteria under which the bank could suspend all trading activities of the partnership and force immediate liquidation. Citibank also has the exclusive right to book all transactions of the partnership. Besides the obvious benefit of generating fees for Citibank, this feature of the arrangement provides a means for close monitoring of the partnership's activities.

This third-party guarantee offers several advantages over the earlier variety. First of all, it provides greater protection for the investor, making the resulting package clearly superior to convertible debt. Perhaps more important, such a third-party guarantee also resolves informational asymmetry costs in an efficient manner. The bank or other guarantor has economies of scale and scope that reduce the cost of processing complex information about the entity issuing the puttable equity. Such services, if competitively priced, could resolve a significant problem in the IPO market.

SUMMARY

Puttable stock has been devised to resolve problems arising from the need to raise equity capital when management believes that the market price of ordinary common stock is too low (that is, when there are significant informational asymmetry costs). Although puttable stock is a relatively new financial innovation it offers promise as a potential means to reduce the underpricing problem for initial public offerings. For a young company seeking funds to finance growth, puttable stock also offers a publicly traded alternative to a mezzanine debt financing, in which the lender receives warrants to buy common stock.[18] Whether or not puttable stock financing is the long-sought solution to the underpricing of IPOs remains to be seen. There is theoretical justification for believing that it can be a solution, and the Arley case provides tantalizing, though tentative, empirical verification.

Puttable stock may also offer a solution for problems faced by companies that have already gone public but need to raise new common equity in the face of high informational asymmetry costs. Because of its potential ability to solve significant problems, therefore, puttable stock deserves to be considered a worthwhile experiment and tried more extensively.

A puttable stock is similar to a convertible bond from the investors' perspective, but with several additional benefits to the issuer. The options allowing the issuer to choose cash, notes, preferred stock, or common stock as the means for meeting the guarantee provide an efficient alternative to bankruptcy proceedings. Such provisions may therefore reduce the expected "bankruptcy" costs and therefore enhance the market value of the corporation. In addition, such provisions allow management to mitigate the cost of informational asymmetries that might exist at the time the puts mature.

If puttable stock is to be effective, holders must be adequately protected from possible attempts to welsh on the guarantee. Therefore it is necessary that well-thought-out default mechanisms be provided in the arrangement. When the issuer retains protection from early exercise, furthermore, restrictions on the payment of dividends will be necessary to protect the holders of puttable stock from potential wealth transfers. In the absence of such antiwelshing protection, potential investors will have to protect themselves by anticipating the worst and offering a correspondingly lower price for the puttable stock issue. Thus, just as in the case of restrictive covenants in bond contracts, the appropriate restrictions benefit both the holders of puttable stock (in the form of reduced risk) and the founding shareholders (in the form of a lower cost of capital for financing the firm's expansion).

Puttable stock was devised to resolve problems arising from the need to raise equity capital under adverse conditions (that is, significant informational asymmetry costs). When debt financing is an acceptable alternative, zero-coupon convertible bonds, such as liquid yield option notes (LYONs), may be a more attractive alternative for issuers with established capital bases and an established stream of taxable income. Convertible exchangeable preferred (CEP) stock is another alternative for well-established companies that offers a similar basic arrangement with specialized advantages. CEP is dividend-paying preferred stock that is convertible at the option of the holder into common stock, and exchangeable at the option of the issuer into convertible bonds.

A common feature of CEP issues is that the issuer must wait a specified time (usually two years, but sometimes three) before being able to exchange the preferred stock for convertible bonds. The bonds are defined as having a face value equal to the par value of the preferred stock, carry a coupon rate equal to the dividend rate of the preferred, and are subordinate to other existing debt. Each bond, furthermore, is convertible into common stock on a basis identical to the conversion feature of the preferred stock. In every way except for tax purposes, that is, the convertible bonds are identical to the preferred stock. We can account for several billion dollars of CEP issues in recent years.

APPENDIX 3A

This appendix shows a simplified version of Ingersoll's valuation model of convertible bonds using the Black-Scholes option pricing model (OPM).

Black and Scholes (1973) have pointed out that the option pricing model can be used to evaluate the common equity and debt of a levered firm. Assume that a firm has in its capital structure a nonconvertible discount debt and common equity. The payoffs to the bondholders and the equityholders at the maturity date of the debt can be shown as follows:

$$Y_B = \begin{cases} B & \text{if } V_T \geq B \\ V_T & \text{otherwise} \end{cases}$$

$$= \min [B, V_T], \tag{1}$$

and

$$Y_E = \begin{cases} V_T - B & \text{if } V_T > B \\ 0 & \text{otherwise} \end{cases}$$

$$= \max [V_T - B, 0], \tag{2}$$

where

Y_B = payoff to the bondholders at maturity date

Y_E = payoff to the equityholders at maturity date

V_T = total value of the firm at maturity date

B = total promised payment of the debt

It is clear from the expression in Equation (2) that the common equity of a levered firm can be viewed as a call option—an option for the shareholders to purchase the firm from the bondholders at the maturity date of the debt for an exercise price equal to the total promised payment of the bond. Therefore, with this interpretation, one can easily apply the Black-Scholes OPM to determine the value of the firm's common stock, S, as follows:

$$S = VN(d_1) - Be^{-rt} N(d_2) \tag{3}$$

where

V = current total value of the firm

r = risk-free rate of interest

T = time to maturity of the bond

d_1 = $[\ln (V/B) + (r + \frac{\sigma^2}{2}) T] / \sigma \sqrt{T}$

$d_2 = d_1 - \sigma \sqrt{T}$

σ^2 = variance rate of the firm's total value

$N(\cdot)$ = cumulative normal probability density function

e = exponential function

Since the value of debt is simply the total value of the firm minus the value of common stock, we can use the OPM to derive the value of the firm's risky discount bond, D, as follows:

$$D = V - S$$

$$= V[1 - N(d_1)] + Be^{-rT}N(d_2). \qquad (4)$$

Merton (1974) has analyzed in detail the risk structure of interest rate on corporate bonds using the expression in Equation (4).

As Ingersoll has pointed out, the value of the conversion privilege (CP) of a convertible bond can also be determined using the OPM. In addition to holding a regular discount bond, the holders of a zero-coupon convertible bond have a conversion privilege to convert the debt into a fraction of the firm's common equity. In other words, the holders of the convertible bonds have a call option to purchase a fraction of the firm's common stock at an exercise price equal to the face value of the bond. Since the debt is convertible for a fraction (α) of the post-conversion equity, α is the dilution factor that indicates the fraction of the common equity that would be held by the bondholders if the entire debt were converted. If there are n shares of common stock outstanding and the debt can be exchanged for N shares in aggregate, then the dilution factor is $\alpha = N/(n + N)$.

Therefore, using the Black-Scholes OPM, the value of the conversion privilege can be determined in the following equation:

$$CP = \alpha VN(b_1) - Be^{-rT}N(b_2) \qquad (5)$$

where

$$b_1 = [\ln(\alpha V/B) + (r + \sigma^2/2) T] / \sigma \sqrt{T}$$
$$b_2 = b_1 - \sigma \quad T$$

As Ingersoll has shown, the value of a zero-coupon convertible bond (CD) is simply the sum of the value of a nonconvertible discount bond and the value of the conversion privilege, and we know that the value of a zero-coupon convertible bond should be:

$$CD = D + CP$$

$$= V[1 - N(d_1)] + Be^{-rT}N(d_2) + \alpha VN(b_1) - Be^{-rT}N(b_2). \tag{6}$$

Therefore, Equation (6) indicates that the Black-Scholes OPM can be employed to determine the value of a zero-coupon convertible bond. The first term of the right-hand side of the equation represents the value of a nonconvertible discount bond and the second term represents the value of the conversion privilege.

As shown in this chapter, a puttable stock is equivalent to a zero-coupon convertible bond. The procedure of using the Black-Scholes OPM to evaluate a zero-coupon convertible bond can be used to determine the value of a puttable stock.

NOTES

1. Details on the case of Arley Merchandise Corporation are reported in Claire Makin, "The Boom in Uncommon Stock," pp. 101-2.

2. Cash settlements were promised to small shareholders, but holders of large blocks could be paid off in senior subordinated notes paying 128 percent of the ten-year Treasury bond rate.

3. Lest this be seen as a simple case of "greenmail," it should be noted that Smith took a loss of $85 million even at this premium price. Smith paid $165 million for its stake in Gearhart (an average price of $31 per share) more than a year earlier and mounted a serious effort to merge with Gearhart. Gearhart's founder and chief executive, Marvin Gearhart, fought hard and successfully to remain independent. Meanwhile the price of oil plummeted, casting a pall over the oil-field services industry.

4. The Gearhart offering was announced in *The Wall Street Journal* on March 28, 1985, p. 45.

5. Under the terms of the agreement, redeeming a right for cash, notes, or preferred stock required that a share of common stock be surrendered at the time of exercise. No such surrender would be required, however, when exercising a right for additional shares of common stock.

6. The offering price was $75 per unit ($15 per share). The exercise price per share was set at $21.68 five years after issue (June 1990). Limited opportunities for early exercise were provided at annual intervals, during the last 15 business days in June. During each of these exercise windows, Gearhart was required to honor only 20 percent of the outstanding puts, on a first-come, first-served basis. Exercise prices for early exercise were set by the prospectus at $14.68, $16.18, $17.84, and $19.67 in 1986, '87, '88, and '89, respectively. This graduated scale reflects an increase of 10 percent compounded semiannually.

7. The daily returns for the S&P 500 were deducted from the daily returns for Gearhart to calculate the market-adjusted residual. These daily residuals were then cumulated over the period from March 4 to May 3, 1985.

8. Although a home-made "synthetic protective put" can be created by using a dynamic asset allocation scheme, the high transaction costs will prevent individual investors from using such a strategy.

9. An ordinary put is an option that is issued by a party other than the issuer of the underlying common stock, such as those traded on the Chicago Board Options Exchange (CBOE).

10. There is no "standard" puttable stock contract. A variety of terms and conditions can be laid out in any given puttable stock prospectus, but the essential elements are simple. A puttable stock unit contains one put for each share of common stock, and the issuer must be able to satisfy all obligations by issuing more shares of common stock if the puts are exercised. To our knowledge, no puttable stock issues have provided the issuer with a recall privilege. The analysis in this section focuses on the most basic situation. Later in the chapter we consider the rationale for providing the issuer with alternate means of meeting the obligations arising from the puts (i.e., cash, notes, or preferred stock).

11. The exact method for determining the number of shares may vary from case to case, and must be described clearly in the prospectus, just as in convertible bond arrangements. In the Gearhart case, for example, the number of additional shares would be calculated by a formula that establishes the "market value" as 90 percent of the average market price for the 60 days prior to the exercise period. Since the terms of the puts are publicly available information, it is reasonable to expect that the market price of the stock reflects the expected dilution effects.

12. Hans Stoll, "The Relationship Between Put and Call," pp. 801–824, and Robert Merton, "Theory of Rational Option Pricing," pp. 141–83,

established the put-call parity relationship for European options written on underlying assets with a variety of return-generating functions. A call plus the present value of the exercise price (discounted at the T-bill rate) is equivalent to the underlying asset plus a put. Expressed symbolically: $C(V,G,t) + Ge^{-rt} = V + P(V,G,t)$. Under the assumptions listed above, this relationship can be applied in our analysis. The owners of puttable stock hold $\alpha V + P(\alpha V,G,t) - P(V,G,t)$. By transforming the two puts into their equivalents, it can be shown that this equals $V - C(V,G,t) + C(\alpha V,G,t)$, which is Ingersoll's valuation model for zero-coupon convertible bonds. That is, the holders of the convertible bonds own the whole firm and are short a call to sell it for G, but have another call to buy an α share of it for G—which works out to be the same package of claims held by the owners of puttable stock.

13. The daily returns for the S&P 500 were deducted from the daily returns for Arley to calculate the market-adjusted residual. These daily residuals were then cumulated over the period from November 15, 1984 to June 28, 1985.

14. The exact wording of the prospectus is as follows: "Any Preferred Stock [exchanged for rights] will pay noncumulative cash dividends at a rate equal to the highest quarterly cash dividend rate for the Common Stock from the issuance date of the Rights to the issuance of such Preferred Stock, will have a specified liquidation preference, will be optionally redeemable at any time at liquidation value, will be convertible on a one-for-one basis into Common Stock and will vote together with the Common Stock except as otherwise required by applicable law."

15. It is worth noting that the founding shareholders will not be disenfranchised completely, although their stake in the firm may be reduced to a very small one. In the situation of a small startup company this can provide valuable incentives to the founders, whose continued efforts are critical to the success of the venture.

16. This criterion for a worthwhile financial innovation was set forth by James Van Horne, "Of Financial Innovations," pp. 621–31.

17. In 1975 the Financial Accounting Standards Board and the Securities and Exchange Commission banned the use of the deferral, or capitalization, method of accounting for R&D expenditures and required expensing by all firms.

18. Mezzanine loans are similar to convertible bonds when, as is commonly the case, the lender receives warrants to purchase common stock. In the case of a young company that has attractive growth potential but has not yet established a steady cash flow, the lender may extend an additional line of credit upon which the borrower can draw to make interest payments. In such a case, the mezzanine loan is much like a zero-coupon convertible bond.

REFERENCES

Beatty, Randolph, and Jay Ritter. "Investment Banking, Reputation, and the Underpricing of Initial Public Offerings," *Journal of Financial Economics* 15 (1986), pp. 213–32.

Black, Fischer, and Myron Scholes. "The Pricing of Options and Corporate Liabilities." *Journal of Political Economy* 81 (May-June 1973): pp. 637–59.

Horowitz, B., and R. Kolodny. "The FASB, the SEC, and R&D," *Bell Journal of Economics* 12 (Spring 1981), pp. 249–62.

Ingersoll, Jonathan, Jr., "A Contingent-Claims Valuation of Convertible Securities," *Journal of Financial Economics* 5 (1977), pp. 289–322.

Leland, Hayne, and David Pyle. "Informational Asymmetries, Financial Structure, and Financial Intermediation," *Journal of Finance* 32 (May 1977), pp. 371–87.

Makin, Claire. "The Boom in Uncommon Stock," *Institutional Investor* (June 1985), pp. 101–02.

Merton, Robert. "Theory of Rational Option Pricing," *Bell Journal of Economics and Management Science* 4 (1973), pp. 141–83.

Merton, Robert. "On the Pricing of Corporate Debt: The Risk Structure of Interest Rates," *Journal of Finance* 29 (May 1974), pp. 449–70.

Ritter, Jay. "The Costs of Going Public," *Journal of Financial Economics* 19 (1987), pp. 269–81.

Rock, Kevin. "Why New Issues are Underpriced," *Journal of Financial Economics* 15 (1986), pp. 187–212.

Shapiro, Alan. "Corporate Strategy and the Capital Budgeting Decision," *Midland Corporate Finance Journal* 3 (Spring 1985), pp. 22–36.

Stoll, Hans. "The Relationship Between Put and Call Option Prices," *Journal of Finance* 24 (December 1969), pp. 801–24.

Van Horne, James. "Of Financial Innovations and Excesses," *Journal of Finance* 40 (July 1985), pp. 621–31.

Chapter 4

Tax-Deductible Equity

It is only natural that innovative financial managers who desire the advantages of equity financing without having to give up the tax advantages of debt will try to design financing methods that are equivalent to tax-deductible equity. It is also natural that alert tax authorities and other regulators will try to thwart them. The continuing interplay of financial managers and regulators leads to an ever-changing array of financing innovations. This process of action and reaction represents a specific instance of what has been termed the "regulatory dialectic," in which those being regulated seek new loopholes while the regulators endeavor to close the most heavily exploited ones.[1]

This chapter first describes three recent attempts to gain the advantages of tax-deductible equity, which were quickly squelched by regulators, then discusses a recent reversal of the familiar roles, in which Congress itself provided a new opportunity for tax-deductible equity financing under the Tax Reform Act (TRA) of 1984. This benefit came from changes made to encourage the formation and expansion of employee stock ownership plans (ESOPs). These changes became fully effective only at the beginning of 1985.

THREE RECENT SHORT-LIVED ATTEMPTS TO CREATE TAX-DEDUCTIBLE EQUITY

During the early 1980s, some very innovative attempts to create tax-deductible equity came to light. The first one to be discussed is the so-called "leveraged preferred financing" used by some major utility companies to finance their new construction. The passage of the Tax Reform Act in 1984, however, quickly squelched this method of financing. The next section describes the "tax-deductible preferred" arrangement created by officials at Continental Illinois Bank and Dean Witter Reynolds, Inc.[2] It was used by Midland-Ross Corporation and IU International Corporation, but quickly fell prey to unfavorable FASB and SEC rulings. Last, the "adjustable rate convertible notes" (ARCNs) innovated by Goldman, Sachs & Company are described.[3] ARCNs were used by Nicor Inc. to raise $45 million and by Borg Warner Corporation to raise $100 million in late 1982. Then, in early 1983, ARCNs were used to raise $50 million by MAPCO and $80 million by Hercules, Inc. ARCNs were terminated by a June 1983 IRS ruling.

Leveraged Preferred Financing

One of the tax-deduction ploys specifically eliminated in the TRA of 1984 was the financial arrangements in which preferred corporations borrowed money to buy preferred stock. Through such transactions, leverage was used to magnify the benefits of the 85 percent dividends-received exclusion on preferred stock. In some instances, complex private placements were used to pass part of the tax advantages back to the corporation issuing the preferred stock. Although the tax deductions on interest payments were actually taken by someone else, part of the advantage could be passed back to the issuer through a dividend on the preferred stock, which was set lower than the prevailing market rate. Indirectly, the issuer got part of the tax advantages and created a tax-deductible equity.

There were three principal participants in the leveraged preferred financing arrangement:[4] (1) an issuer of preferred stock
(referred to below as the issuing corporation), (2) a group of
investors acting as equity participants, and (3) a group of institutional lenders to purchase the debt position in the transaction.
These participants were brought together by means of two trust
arrangements: (1) an owner-trust, established by the equity
participants for the purpose of acquiring the preferred stock and
issuing the debt (trust-secured notes), and (2) a lender-trust,
established for the benefit of the lenders, which was to hold the
preferred stock as collateral.

Upon closing of the leveraged preferred financing, the trust
arrangements were crystallized into contractual obligations by the
formation of the preferred corporation, which administered the
disbursements. Formed on the basis of the capital put up by the
equity participants, it sold debt instruments to the lenders. The
issuing corporation wrote redeemable preferred stock to be
purchased by the preferred corporation. The loans to the preferred corporation were secured solely by the preferred stock and
an assignment of all payments thereon.

The advantage for the equity holders was that they received,
not only the tax deduction from the interest on the debt, but the
85 percent dividend exclusion on the entire issue of preferred
stock. This was possible because of the trust arrangements in the
leveraged preferred financing. For tax purposes, the equity
participants, through the owner's trust, "received" all the dividend payments on the preferred stock and "paid" all the interest
on the loan. Ideally, the preferred corporation's pretax dividend
receipts were just enough to cover its pretax interest payments.
Although no cash would go directly from the trust to the equity
participants in such a case, they would be able to take a deduction
for all of the interest while paying tax on only 15 percent of the
dividends. Thus, for tax purposes, their losses exceeded their
income from the arrangement. In the ideal situation, the equity
participants would experience no change in their pretax cash flow
but would enjoy a lower tax bill.

A specific example will illustrate the arrangement. In April 1982, a leveraged preferred financing was constructed around a $50 million par value issue of 12.31 percent cumulative redeemable preferred stock by a major utility company. The proceeds were used to finance the utility's ongoing construction program. Because of the tax advantages they received, the equity participants allowed the utility to issue preferred stock at 50 to 75 basis points below what the utility's executives believed to be the prevailing market rate for preferred stock of equivalent risk. The trust arrangements were set up to buy the issue of preferred stock and subsequently to place two issues of debt: $32.1 million of 16.75 percent senior secured notes due in 1998 and $4.5 million of 17 percent subordinated secured notes due in 1992. Thus, the annual payments (through 1992) were 16.78 percent of the total of $36.6 million raised from debt participants. The remaining $13.4 million was provided by the equity participants.

The after-tax spread of 2.40 percent between dividends received and interest paid (with a 46 percent tax rate), after being leveraged, contributed to the equity participants' overall yield of 18.01 percent after tax.[5] The debt participants incurred a higher level of risk and consequently higher return in this arrangement than would have been the case if first-mortgage bonds had been used to finance the same construction. They also had the opportunity to share in the tax benefits of the leveraged preferred arrangement by negotiating higher interest rates on the privately placed bonds than would normally be available to the public in investments of equivalent risk.

Tax-Deductible Preferred Stock

The tax-deductible preferred stock introduced by Continental Illinois Bank and Dean Witter Reynolds also utilized a trust arrangement. The issuing corporation "sold" the stock to a wholly owned trust, set up with equity capital provided by the issuing corporation. The trust then borrowed against future dividends, pledging the preferred stock as sole security. The IRS took the position that as long as dividends were being paid into the trust, the issuing corporation was in effect paying dividends to itself. Therefore, the dividends were not treated as taxable income for anyone. The IRS recognized only the debt support payments being made by the trust subsidiary and allowed the deduction of interest by the parent.

The innovators hoped that the FASB and the SEC would allow the transaction to be carried on the issuer's books as equity. The argument for doing so was that, in the event the issuer was unable to pay dividends, the terms of the loan allowed the trust to turn over the stock to the lenders as full settlement of the debt. Thus, in the event of financial distress, the creditors would become stockholders. It could, therefore, be argued that the debt arising from the arrangement endangered neither existing nor future creditors of the issuer. In February 1985, however, the FASB and SEC announced that the parent and subsidiary should be consolidated for accounting purposes. The arrangement would have to be carried on the issuer's books as debt.

Despite the required accounting treatment, the arrangement may still be attractive to some issuers of preferred stock. It does provide the tax-deductibility of debt with a valuable safety feature, because the debt turns into equity automatically in the event of financial distress. As long as the rate of return on the loan is just sufficient to compensate the lenders for the risks they bear, the only loser in this arrangement is the U.S. Treasury.

Adjustable-Rate Convertible Notes

Adjustable-rate convertible notes were squelched by the IRS in 1983. They were created in an attempt to exploit a gap in IRS regulations concerning the distinction between debt and equity. The ARCNs were called debt instruments by their issuers but were convertible at any time into common stock at the discretion of the holder. They were also redeemable at the discretion of the issuer in such a way that partial conversion could be forced. Furthermore, the "interest" payments on the notes were pegged to the dividends paid on the common stock of the issuing corporation. Although they were called debt, the ARCNs behaved very much like equity.

The 1983 MAPCO issue is a good illustration. It was a $50 million issue of 20-year $1,000 notes. Each one was convertible into 43.95 shares of MAPCO common stock. This represents a conversion price of $22.75, which was the price of MAPCO common stock at the time. The quarterly interest payments on the notes were pegged to common stock dividends. The holder of a single note received the higher of either $22.50 (representing the quarterly installment of a 9 percent annual interest rate) or that quarter's common stock cash dividend multiplied by 43.95 (to reflect the conversion ratio), plus an extra amount of $2.75. The quarterly payment was capped at $50 per note.

Because of the guaranteed minimum payment of $22.50 and the extra $2.75 added to the cash dividends, there was a disincentive for the holder to convert. As long as the tax authorities allowed the deduction of the "interest" payments on the note, MAPCO had an incentive to minimize the attractiveness of conversion. Managers of MAPCO made the notes redeemable to provide a chance of getting out of the arrangement in the event of a change in tax policy or some other calamity. The cash redemption price was $550. The remaining $450 of the note's face value would be paid in common stock at the conversion ratio. The details of the redemption feature were the key to the tax loophole the issuers hoped to exploit. The cash redemption payment was 55 percent of a note's face value, and the common stock payment was 45 percent of face value. Therefore, MAPCO representatives could argue that, for accounting purposes, the notes are a hybrid security with a 55 percent debt component and a 45 percent equity component. For tax purposes, however, they hoped that the whole issue would be treated as debt by the IRS. In June 1983, however, the IRS issued a ruling that ARCNs would be treated as equity, and hence that their interest payments were not tax-deductible.

THE LEVERAGED ESOP

The Tax Reform Act (TRA) of 1984 included provisions that encourage the formation of employee stock ownership plans (ESOPs). Companies can now deduct from taxable income any dividends they pay to an ESOP. Moreover, when an ESOP borrows to purchase the common stock of an employer corporation, the lender is now required to pay tax on only half of the interest income from that loan.[6] Because of these incentives, selling its stock to an ESOP can be an attractive way for a corporation to raise tax-deductible common equity.[7]

The Arrangement

The basic arrangement is clarified in the illustration at the end of the chapter. There need be only three principal participants in the arrangement: the employer corporation, the lender, and the ESOP. An ESOP trust borrows from the lender on behalf of the ESOP and buys common stock from the employer corporation. The trust subsequently services the debt from dividends and contributions that the employer pays into it. Such dividends are fully tax-deductible, and other contributions are deductible up to a maximum of 25 percent of payroll.[8] In effect, then, it is possible for principal as well as interest payments to be tax-deductible for the employer corporation. Moreover, the tax-deduction benefit is in addition to the benefit of the low interest cost that may be made possible by the favorable tax treatment given to the lender.[9] As the debt is retired, shares of stock are taken out of the trust and credited to the participants' accounts in the ESOP.

As far as the employer corporation is concerned, it has equity financing and will be making tax-deductible payments to service it. In case the employer is unable to make sufficient payments into the trust to enable it to service the debt, the lender would have recourse only to the assets held in trust for the employee stock ownership plan.

Protection for the Lender

The tax incentives to the lender may not be enough to induce it to make a loan to the ESOP, because the resources for repayment are limited to the dividends and contributions paid into the trust by the employer corporation. A very simple remedy would be for the employer corporation to guarantee the loan, backing it with its full faith and credit. Then, however, the financing arrangement would not be equivalent to tax-deductible equity, because the lender would have recourse to the assets of the employer. A possible compromise would be for a separately incorporated subsidiary of the employer corporation to guarantee the loan, with the lender agreeing to limited recourse in case of default. Such a subsidiary might exist in the form of a trust, formed solely for the purpose of holding as collateral an agreed-upon set of assets passed to it by the parent.

Another way for the employer corporation to enhance the safety of the ESOP's debt is to contribute additional common stock to the ESOP, over and above the shares purchased with the proceeds from the loan. Such a contribution, up to 25 percent of the annual payroll, would be tax-deductible.[10]

Analysis of the Tax Advantage

The net advantage of a leveraged ESOP can be calculated by comparing the net present value of selling stock to the public with the net present value of selling stock to the ESOP. If we denote V as the present value of a new investment to be financed by selling additional common stocks, the net present value of selling stock to the public will be:

$$NPVSP = V - PVDS \qquad (1)$$

where,

NPVSP = the net present value of selling stock to the public

PVDS　　= 　the present value of the dividend stream associated with the stock.

The net present value of selling stock to the leveraged ESOP will be:

$$NPVSEP = V - (1 - t)\, PVDS - (1 - t)\, PVC \qquad (2)$$

where,

NPVSEP　=　the net present value of selling stock to the leveraged ESOP

t　　　　=　the marginal corporate income tax rate

PVC　　=　the present value of contributions to the ESOP.

Therefore, subtracting Equation (1) from Equation (2) gives the net advantage (NA) of selling stock to the leveraged ESOP as:

$$NA = tPVDS - (1 - t)\, PVC \qquad (3)$$

We have illustrated the net advantage of selling stock to the leveraged ESOP in Exhibit 6 below.

SUMMARY

In the recent past, there have been ingenious financing innovations designed to gain the elusive but very attractive goal of tax-deductible equity financing. We have described three that quickly fell prey to the regulatory dialectic and were squelched by the authorities. Ironically, the very same legislation (the TRA of 1984) that eliminated the leveraged preferred financing arrangement also provided the opportunity for leveraged ESOPs. Furthermore, there is a variation on the leveraged ESOP that is very similar to the short-lived leveraged preferred financing arrangement.

Exhibit 6
An Illustration of the Tax Incentives for ESOP Financing

The net advantage of selling stock to a leveraged ESOP is equal to the tax savings from the dividend deduction (plus any tax credit earned), minus the after-tax present value of the contributions to the ESOP. It can be illustrated by comparing the net present value of selling stock to the public with the net present value of selling stock to the ESOP.

Assume an ESOP buys $100 million of qualified securities (one million shares of common stock at $100 per share), borrowing the full $100 million with the employer's guarantee. The loan is to be amortized over ten equal annual payments as an ordinary annuity discounted at 10 percent interest. Under these assumptions, the annual loan payment would be $16.27 million before tax. Because the lender pays tax on only half of the interest income, the after-tax rate of return on the loan would be 8.30 percent, making this loan just as profitable as a non-ESOP loan earning 12.58 percent before tax. Since the annual payments at that rate would be $18.12 million, this incentive saves the borrower almost $2 million per year over the life of the loan.

Suppose the current dividend is $5 per share and that without the ESOP financing there would be no change expected in the future dividend stream, so the current stock price of $100 per share implies that the cost of equity capital is 15 percent. The annual dividend payment to the ESOP is expected to be $15 million, so the employer would be required to make an additional annual contribution of $1.27 million to the ESOP for the next ten years. At the current 34 percent marginal corporate income tax rate, the dividend deduction will save the employer $5.1 million per year in taxes, which represents new equity capital. The after-tax annual contribution to the ESOP will be only $838,200, and will be finished after ten years. The present value of the tax savings on the dividend payments is $34 million, while the after-tax present value of the annual contribution of $1.27 million to the ESOP for ten years (discounted at the 15 percent cost of equity capital) is $4.2 million. Therefore, the net advantage of selling stock to the leveraged ESOP is $29.8 million. When the loan is repaid, the proceeds from investing the tax savings will allow a dividend increase for all stockholders.

Thus, all the participants in the arrangement stand to benefit at the expense of the U.S. Treasury. The employees build wealth through participation in the ESOP. The lender gets an attractive after-tax yield even if the loan is made at a rate that is below the market interest rate. The employer gets the opportunity to raise equity funds that enjoy tax-deductible payments. Finally, the former stockholders get cash which they are free to reinvest as they like.

Besides the tax benefits, the leveraged ESOP offers additional potential benefits through possible improved employee morale and the willingness of the employees (in light of the wealth accumulating for them in the ESOP) to work for a lower level of cash compensation. There is also the possibility that ownership of a significant portion of the common stock by the ESOP might make it more challenging for an outsider to take over the employer corporation.

NOTES

1. E. Kane, "Good Intentions and Unintended Evil," pp. 55–69, used the term "regulatory dialectic" in a paper on credit allocation. In it, he said, "introducing political power into economic affairs initiates a dialectical process of adjustments and counter-adjustments. In what resembles reflex action, markets rechannel regulatory power, as regulators short-circuit regulator intentions . . . by finding and exploiting loopholes."

2. This arrangement was reported in *The Wall Street Journal*, December 26, 1984, p. 4. Its difficulties with the regulators were reported shortly afterward in *The Wall Street Journal*, February 21, 1985, p. 46.

3. This arrangement was reported in J. W. Friar, "Blending Debt and Equity." Its demise was reported in *The Wall Street Journal*, June 27, 1983, p. 20.

4. The leveraged preferred financing arrangement is discussed in more detail in Andrew Chen and John Kensinger, "A New Wrinkle in Corporate Finance."

5. The yield is calculated as follows: The equity participants received dividends of $6,155,000 annually, of which only $923,250 was taxable. At a 46 percent marginal income tax rate, they paid $424,695 in tax, leaving them $5,730,305 after tax. They were scheduled to pay interest of $6,141,750 annually before tax, which is only $3,316,545 after tax. The spread between after-tax dividends and interest was $2,413,760. This is 18.01 percent of the $13.4 million equity investment.

The pretax dividends were only slightly more than the pretax debt support payments. Thus, the trusts that made up the preferred corporation had a net cash flow near zero. The value of the arrangement for the equity participants arose because they were allowed to consolidate the owner trust's accounts with their own for tax purposes. While the dividends added to their taxable income, the interest payments generated a much larger deduction. The excess deduction could then be used to reduce taxable income from other sources.

6. Tax Reform Act of 1984, Sections 542 and 543.

7. The deductibility of dividends and the favorable tax treatment on the loan are new incentives for the formation of ESOPs. There were other incentives already in existence prior to the TRA of 1984. Contributions paid by an employer to an ESOP are deductible, up to 25 percent of payroll (see note 8). There is also a tax credit on contributions (see note 11).

8. Internal Revenue Code, Section 415, paragraph 19,566.

9. At a 46 percent marginal corporate tax rate, the lender would be able to give 30 percent discount on the interest rate charged and still receive the same after-tax income from the loan to the ESOP as from an ordinary loan. To show this, let π = the rate charged to ordinary customers in the same risk class, and P = the rate charged to the ESOP. The after-tax rate or return from the ordinary loan is 0.54 π, and that for the ESOP loan is $(1-0.46)(0.5)P = 0.77P$. Equating after-tax returns and solving for P yields $P = 0.7013\ \pi$.

10. Internal Revenue Code, Section 415, paragraph 19,566.

REFERENCES

Chen, Andrew, and John Kensinger. "A New Wrinkle in Corporate Finance: Leveraged Preferred Financing," Working Paper 84-301, Edwin L. Cox School of Business, SMU, 1984.

Chen, Andrew, and John Kensinger. "Innovations in Corporate Financing: Tax-Deductible Equity," *Financial Management* (Winter 1985), pp. 44–51.

Friar, J. W. "Blending Debt and Equity," *Institutional Investor* (May 1983).

Kane, E. "Good Intentions and Unintended Evil: The Case Against Selective Credit Allocation," *Journal of Money, Credit and Banking* (February 1977), pp. 55–69.

Newspapers

"IRS Rules That Notes Convertible into Stock Are Equity, Not Debt," *The Wall Street Journal* (June 27, 1983), p. 20.

"Regulators Squelch Firms' New Method for Issuing Preferred," *The Wall Street Journal* (February 21, 1985), p. 46.

"Search for Corporate Financing Lead to Tax-Deductible Equity—and Debate," *The Wall Street Journal* (December 26, 1984), p. 4.

Chapter 5

Beyond the Tax Effects of Employee Stock Ownership

The preceding chapter described the tax incentives for employee stock ownership plan (ESOP) financing. Such tax incentives constitute a sizable burden for the federal government. In fiscal 1986, their cost to the government totaled $2.5 billion; if current trends continue, the total cost is projected to reach $4.4 billion in 1990.[1] What gave rise to the costly ESOP financing? ESOPs arose about 30 years ago out of the controversial theories of Louis Kelso, who established the first such plan himself at a California newspaper. He found a powerful political ally in Louisiana's Russell Long, chairman of the Senate Finance Committee. With Long's help, ESOPs were officially endorsed by a series of legislative acts and adopted by many companies from 1974 to 1986. Senator Long retired in 1986, however, and a new ally with his combination of commitment and clout will be hard to find. Since Long's retirement, legislators have shown that they will be very discriminating as they decide whether to maintain the existing incentive structure.

The number of corporations with ESOPs has increased very rapidly since this method of financing began. In 1975 there were only about 1,200 corporations with ESOPs. At present there exist approximately 8,000, with 8 million employees participating.[2] These numbers yield an average of about 1,000 employees per plan. However, this number is deceptively high due to distortion by a few very large plans. Most of the corporations having ESOPs are small, and only a handful of them have ever been publicly traded. In a recent survey of 188 large companies conducted by Towers Perrin, moreover, it was found that 75 percent lack ESOPs. Most companies do not want them, the survey found, and only 12 percent of those with ESOPs reported taking full advantage of the associated tax benefits.[3]

It seems surprising at first that more corporate giants have not taken advantage of the tax incentives for ESOP financing, but there may be good reasons for wariness. If taxpayers aren't getting their money's worth, the incentives will be taken away, and those who jumped on the band wagon too hastily may be left high and dry. Besides, it is questionable for corporate managers to make a major change for tax reasons only. What is needed is good economic justification as well.

So what else is there to recommend ESOP financing? There are two potential nontax pluses for ESOP financing, one well known and one less apparent. The first is the potential for enhanced productivity through better employee motivation. The second is enhanced market control over reinvestment of corporate cash flows. Besides giving employees a chance for an ownership stake in their companies, ESOPs put cash into the hands of stockholders, who proceed to make the reinvestment decisions themselves. Over the next several years, leveraged ESOPs commit the firm's cash flows to debt retirement and divert the funds from cash cows into the marketplace, where they can nourish the highest-valued new ventures.

On the negative side, there are some potentially damaging problems that result from lack of diversification. And there are those who would use ESOPs to "save" dying operations, thwart takeovers, or entrench privileged groups.

SOME ESOPS WORK, BUT SOME DON'T

Consider the following "optimistic" scenario: Employees who have labored long and hard are offered the chance to emulate great capitalists by borrowing money to buy their employer, pledging the company's cash flows as collateral for the loan. No longer employed by a faceless group of shareholders, they work for themselves— harder than ever before. They pay off the loan in a few years and then prosper.

This optimistic scenario has a real-life counterpart in the very successful employee ownership plan at W. L. Gore & Associates, Inc., of Newark, Delaware. Gore makes Teflon-based materials for vascular grafts as well as Gore-tex, the advanced insulating fabric used in linings for NASA spacesuits and top-of-the-line ski clothing. Employees are named "associates" and senior employees are referred to as "group leaders" or "area leaders" rather than supervisors. A family atmosphere seems to pervade the workplace. Some employees with 15 years of service have accumulated $100,000 or more from the plan.[4] The O&O supermarket chain in Philadelphia is another such story. Formerly a money-losing division of A&P, the chain has made a turnaround that is attributed to the incentives of employee ownership. Likewise, National Steel's Weirton plant was saved from closing by an ESOP in January 1984. The plant has since then shown profits for ten quarters. And employee ownership succeeded in transforming troubled Bridgeport Brass (Connecticut) into the successful Seymour Specialty Wire Co.

The scenario is appealing, but it assumes that there are no limits to the potential payoff from hard work and industriousness. In this sense the optimistic scenario is perhaps one-sided. Therefore, consider a "pessimistic" scenario: An aging company operating a dingy, red-brick factory has employed townspeople from the surrounding communities for generations. Over the years, the employees' union has won a middle-class lifestyle for its members, but now the employees fear for the future. Foreign competitors with cheap labor are undercutting prices and taking market share. The price of the company's stock has plunged, and corporate raiders on the prowl are threatening to liquidate the company. In an effort to save their jobs, employees put up their pension assets and borrow heavily in order to buy their company's stock. Market forces prove impossible to resist, however, and the company continues to wither in the face of competition. Ultimately, the employees still lose their jobs, and the government must bail out their pension plan.

There have been many attempts to use ESOP financing to rescue dying enterprises.[5] In the troubled steel industry, for example, there have been several ESOP bailouts. For instance, an ESOP saved McLouth Steel Corp. from bankruptcy liquidation in exchange for wage concessions. Likewise, LTV arranged to sell its Gadsden, Alabama, plant to employees. In a related industry, Kaiser Aluminum & Chemical Corporation sold a group of 1,200 workers a plant that makes refractory bricks (which are used to line blast furnaces, and face declining demand). Laid-off workers have even entertained the hope of buying and reopening U.S. Steel's Duquesne Works, despite conditions that were eloquently described by one observer as follows:

> The blast furnace stands rusting among overgrown railroad tracks. Pigeons roost in the top of the steelmaking shop. The plant would need a $200 million continuous caster. And nothing can ever be done to remedy its location, hemmed in by the Monongahela River Valley far from deep-water ports.[6]

The tax preferences of ESOP financing, as attractive as they are, cannot overcome the tremendous cost disadvantage that antiquated steel mills face against foreign producers and modern U.S. mills. In the case of declining plants, ESOP financing can do no more than prolong the agony of reducing capacity in overcrowded industries, meanwhile holding back the stronger operations. Some bailouts, moreover, have already gone to the end of the line. In 1979, for example, employees received 60 percent control of Rath Packing Company's aging, inefficient, five-story main plant in Waterloo, Iowa, in exchange for wage concessions. Although the result was remarkable improvements in productivity, worker absenteeism, and grievances, the plant was still compelled by inexorable market forces to close in 1984.

Hyatt-Clark Industries, Inc., came into being in 1981 when an ESOP bought the Clark, New Jersey, ball-bearing plant from General Motors. Despite employee ownership, the union fought constantly with management and finally staged a slowdown, which resulted in lost customers and a reduced workforce.

WHEN IS EMPLOYEE OWNERSHIP MOST BENEFICIAL?

Employee ownership is not a panacea and should not be prescribed indiscriminately. Selling all or part of the company to the employees is feasible only when it resolves existing conflicts between the owners and employees in such a way that both groups are better off.

Employee ownership is certainly not a new thing. Indeed, it is the norm in many sectors of the economy. In the legal and medical professions, for example, sole proprietorship and professional partnership are the predominant organizational forms.[7] This is natural because such a large proportion of productivity is attributable to human capital, which is inherently nonmarketable. Sole proprietorship is also commonplace in agriculture, where despite the extensive use of capital equipment, productivity ultimately depends upon the farmer's willingness and ability to work long, hard hours, even when sick. Wages cannot easily buy such determination. However, employee ownership is not limited to these areas. With the wave of venture capital financing, employee ownership is also becoming widespread in high-tech research, where human capital is again a key component.

ESOPs Don't Always Create Improved Incentives

Advocates of employee ownership argue that an ESOP provides improved motivation, leading to greater effort and less waste. The value of greater effort varies considerably, however. For a star research scientist, the right incentives may make the difference that leads to a great discovery. For a sales representative, incen-

tives may make the difference between a so-so performance and
star quality customer service—which can be worth a lot of money.
For a janitor, however, the potential is considerably less. Careful
focus is called for in making the most of any incentive package,
and ESOPs do not facilitate such focus. Attempts to focus, in
fact, have been squelched by the U.S. Labor Department, which
regulates ESOPs (more on this later).

Even when highly developed human capital is not involved,
however, on-the-job consumption of perks could be reduced by
employee ownership. This works more effectively in small organizations than in large ones, though. Such savings occur only
when the active participants in the business are willing to forego
direct compensation and accept instead an increased equity value.
If, for example, an employee derives $20 worth of satisfaction
from consuming something that costs the employer $100 to
provide, such consumption is inefficient. If the employee had a
25 percent ownership stake and so could realize a $25 increase
in his share of profits from eliminating the perk, he would opt
for more efficient consumption. If the employee had only a
1/1,000th share, however, there would be little incentive to forego
on-the-job consumption.

Employee ownership has potential to enhance value to the
extent that it reduces other conflicts of interest between employees
and owners,[8] but there are limits. Since employees depend upon
their employer for the bulk of their livelihood, they cannot help
having a different set of priorities than outside owners (for whom
the fate of the company affects only a small portion of their total
wealth). For example, when there is a compelling need to reduce
excess capacity in an overcrowded industry, it will be hard for an
increase in the value of one's stake in an ESOP to offset the loss
of a union job.

Another factor is the strength of the labor unions representing
the employees. Consider a capital-intensive firm that has made a
heavy investment in production equipment: the marginal product
of financial capital is large relative to the marginal product of
human capital. A problem would arise for such a firm if the

workers were able to gain a strong bargaining position and take some of the marginal product of financial capital for themselves as wages, benefits, or on-the-job consumption. If anticipated by the capital market, the prospect of such seizures could depress stock values and reduce the inflow of capital into the company. Sale of stock to an ESOP, however, could help resolve the conflict between owners and labor.

In the case of a large capital-intensive operation in combination with a weak labor union, however, there is much less danger that labor will capture a significant part of the return that is due to the owners. Here there is relatively little to be resolved by employee ownership.

ESOPs Lack Diversification

The inherent problem in employee ownership is that it does not permit portfolio diversification. A given amount would be more valuable if contributed to a diversified pension plan portfolio rather than an ESOP.[9] Of course, the problem would be much milder in the case of a large, diversified employer corporation than in the case of a small, technology-intensive firm.

The ability to diversify a portfolio across a broad range of stocks from different companies and industries has generated considerable social benefits by making efficient risk sharing possible. In drilling for oil, for example, putting all of one's wealth into a single well is very risky, whereas spreading that wealth over several wells is much more prudent. This holds true for R&D as well. Committing all of one's wealth to a single research project can be rather dicey, whereas spreading the wealth over a pool of projects is considerably less so. With diversifiable risks neutralized in portfolios, it is possible to mobilize capital for enterprises that otherwise would not be underwritten.

Also, there is reason to believe that having an ESOP will increase the tendency to underinvest in new expansion projects. This prediction is based upon the current understanding of the principal/agent relationship that exists between a corporation's owners and its managers. Management may be less willing to take on risky ventures than the outside shareholders would prefer, because the consequences of failure that are suffered by the managers are more severe than those suffered by the diversified outside shareholders.[10] This difference in risk exposure leads managers to avoid ventures that seem too risky from their own undiversified viewpoint but that are attractive from the diversified viewpoint of outside shareholders. This tendency to pass up good investment opportunities is referred to as the "residual agency cost."[11] Assuring that management's investment decisions are consistent with the desires of outside shareholders would be prohibitively expensive, however, since complete oversight would, in effect, duplicate management's role.

A corporation with an ESOP has decision-makers whose financial well-being is bound even more tightly to the health of their employer. They have tied up, not only their human capital, but their financial capital. Unable to remove any of their wealth from the employer corporation, they are even more prone to underinvest in new growth opportunities or new technologies than are their counterparts in non-ESOP firms (who can at least diversify their financial capital).

Since the market value of a firm reflects, not only the present value of cash flows from established operations, but the present value of growth opportunities,[12] the tendency to underinvest would depress the value of a firm having a large proportion of employee ownership. The underinvestment factor is far less significant for firms in mature industries with relatively few growth opportunities, however, than for firms in young industries where there are many opportunities for growth and assimilation of new technologies.

We can therefore conclude that employee ownership offers the greatest potential gain from enhanced incentives in smaller, human-capital-intensive corporations. However, the lack of diversification exacts its most severe toll in such cases. Therefore, mature, diversified corporations with strong labor unions and few growth opportunities appear to be the best candidates for ESOP financing.

ESOP FINANCING FUNDAMENTALLY ALTERS CORPORATE CONTROL

ESOPs Divert Cash Flows into the Marketplace

The basic arrangement of an ESOP is summarized in Exhibit 7. The reality of ESOP financing is that it transfers control to the marketplace. How does this occur? When the ESOP buys stock from existing shareholders, the latter are immediately free to redeploy the funds into any other ventures they find attractive. They can choose from the full array of opportunities in the capital market. When the employer has guaranteed the loan, the net effect is an immediate return of capital to outside shareholders. The company's future cash flows are impounded to repay the resulting debt. As the debt service payments are made, the lender decides how to reinvest the cash. Thus, cash is forced out of the employer corporation by the ESOP financing.

The tax incentives also work in another way to divert the cash flow out of the company. With the ESOP tax privileges, the corporation can eliminate income tax completely and, in the case of 100 percent ESOP ownership, make its entire pretax cash flow available to retire the trust's debt. Only if such a corporation retained earnings for new investment would there be any need to pay income tax. This is a significant turning of the tables.[13] Traditionally, income tax laws have kept cash inside a company, since paying dividends resulted in double taxation. In the case of a buyout by a leveraged ESOP under current tax rules, the tax penalty is instead levied against retention of earnings for reinvestment. It is therefore better for an ESOP-owned corporation to raise expansion capital by selling new stock to the ESOP rather than retaining earnings. And when this requires the ESOP trust to go to the market for a loan, the growth plans must meet outside scrutiny.

Exhibit 7
How ESOP Financing Works

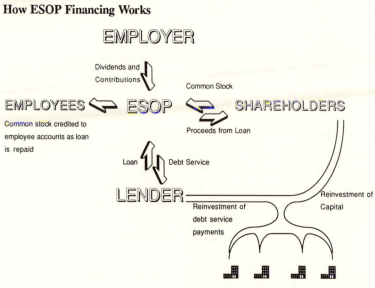

NEW INVESTMENT OPPORTUNITIES

A mature or declining firm may throw off large sums of cash but have few attractive internally generated growth opportunities. Stockholders might worry, therefore, that managers will squander free cash flows[14] on ill-advised attempts to expand the firm into areas in which it lacks experience, expertise, and competitive advantage. Thus, shareholders value any arrangement that commits management to pay out the free cash flows to investors.[15] With creditors to appease, the cash flows are committed to interest and debt retirement for a significant period into the future. New projects would have to compete for external funding rather than being sustained by the employer's cash flows.

In addition to the tax effect, then, the leverage brings with it a change in the process by which management actions are monitored and by which managers are motivated. The burden of debt forces the cash to flow out of the firm rather than circulate within it. If there is any danger that management might not be as demanding in scrutinizing internal investments as the marketplace is, this change increases the probability that the cash flows will find their way to the highest-valued uses. Thus, the economic efficiency is enhanced.

ESOPS AREN'T MEANT TO PROTECT MANAGERS FROM THE UNHAPPY STOCKHOLDERS

Attempts have been made to use ESOP financing to create a protective barrier against corporate raiders. Using ESOP financing as an anti-takeover defense may prove ineffective, however, since the ESOP's shares are held in trust until they are allocated to the employees as the loan is repaid. The trustee—even one appointed by management—has a fiduciary responsibility to the employees and is personally liable for decisions.

After raids by T. Boone Pickens and Carl Icahn, for example, Phillips Petroleum announced plans to form an ESOP that would buy over 30 percent of its common stock for $1.5 billion.[16] Under the Employee Retirement Income Security Act (ERISA), the trustee's primary responsibility is toward securing the retirement income of the employees, but there is leeway to consider the employees' job security. Phillips management, therefore, sought approval of the U.S. Labor Department for a plan that would require the trustee to vote in accordance with the wishes of a majority of participating employees. It was intended that the trustees would vote against any future takeover attempt for fear of losing their jobs. This novel request became irrelevant, however, when Phillips settled with Icahn and tabled the proposed ESOP.

Just as managers can make defensive use of an ESOP, however, a raider can establish an ESOP to form an ally. A successful takeover is not the only way for an outsider to force a change upon management. The recent saga of UAL Corporation, also known as Allegis, is a familiar example. In 1987, United Airlines' parent corporation faced some unusual problems with its own pilots. Rumors of raids further compounded the problem. Richard Ferris, UAL chairman, had worked long and hard to realize his dream of creating a full-range travel services company. He had built a conglomerate whose separate operating divisions included United Airlines, Hertz, Hilton Hotels, and Westin Hotels, with the airline's computerized reservation system at its heart. Much to Ferris' dismay, however, the pilots' union arranged an offer to buy the airline, including the reservations system. An ESOP would pay $4.5 billion.

The pilots made their offer on April 5, 1987. For perspective, the total market value of equity in the whole UAL conglomerate on March 27, 1987 was just under $3 billion ($59 per share). After the offer, the stock commenced a strong upward movement. But the board of directors rejected the bid and the pilots began looking for an ally who would take over the parent company and sell them the airline. The pilots found their friend in Coniston Partners. With the proposed ESOP as a potential buyer for United Airlines, as well as other prospective buyers for Hertz and the corporate hotel properties, Coniston Partners had the leverage they needed to influence the board of directors. Though holding far less than a controlling interest, they threatened a proxy fight, which persuaded the board to repudiate Ferris' strategy, forcing his resignation in June 1987. The stock then edged toward $90 per share, a 50 percent gain in about two months.[17]

ESOPS AREN'T MEANT TO PROTECT ANY PRIVILEGED GROUP FROM MARKET FORCES

The proposed United Airlines ESOP helped overthrow Ferris, allowing investors (and particularly Coniston Partners) to realize a significant increase in value. Its appeal is obvious. At the same time, however, it contains potential disappointment for these same investors. The source of the problem lies in the fact that privileged employees seek to resist the forces of the marketplace that pose a threat to their position. Ultimately, not even the tax subsidies of ESOP financing can prevail in such a quest.

In the case of UAL, pilots and flight attendants have the reputation of being overpaid by industry standards. The head of the pilots' union, moreover, was recently quoted as saying, "We have to control the company from which we draw our salary."[18] Presumably, the object of the pilots' union seeking control of the company is to protect the high payroll and to entrench against the marketplace.

By contrast, the machinists' union claims that its members are being paid at market levels. Thus it has balked. It is becoming increasingly obvious that the deal cannot be struck without the unions' willing participation; yet the union has lost confidence in employee ownership as a result of the unsatisfactory experience with the arrangement at Eastern Airlines. There, despite 25 percent employee ownership, the company was taken over by a staunchly anti-union rival.

There is another, more subtle cause for concern on the machinists' part as well. They fear that the dollars that should be labeled as profits and shared among all employees will go instead to a select few in the form of inflated paychecks. Furthermore, if the pilots and flight attendants were to continue earning more than the industry standard (despite some pay cuts), the airline would be hard-pressed to compete. As a result, job security for all employees would be hurt.

ESOPS AREN'T SUPPOSED TO BE TAX-PRIVILEGED MANAGEMENT BUYOUTS

In order to gain management cooperation, a number of recent ESOPs have given top executives a significantly more attractive deal than that received by other employees. The Dan River ESOP is a case in point. Guided by Kelso & Co. (an investment banking firm specializing in ESOPs), the employees took over the company as a defense against a raid by Carl Icahn in 1983. In the process they created two classes of common stock. A group of top managers put up a relatively small proportion of the total price yet received, not only a disproportionately large stake in the company, but a relatively rich share of the upside potential.[19]

Carl Icahn's threat dissipated, but workers still had little say in running the company. In addition, labor union members continued to be laid off in response to unrelenting pressure from imports. Although Dan River avoided the takeover, control of its cash flow was returned to the marketplace; the necessity of servicing the debt from the employee buyout closed the cash spigot for further investment in the company. This outcome was not welcomed by many employees. After interviews with dozens of them (both hourly and salaried), *Business Week* reported "a near-unanimous feeling that majority ownership has not produced even token democracy in the workplace."[20] The problem at Dan River, however, was really too much for any sort of "employee entrepreneurship" or "workplace democracy" to solve. Dan River was a mature company that could not compete in world markets because in a labor-intensive industry its costs far exceeded those of foreign competitors.

Dan River was not the only situation in which top management received a disproportionate share of equity. In another case, Raymond Industries terminated its pension plan in order to finance an employee buyout, with the intent to repay the loan by what would otherwise have been pension fund contributions. A small management group got half the number of shares as all the other employees for about a twentieth as much investment, along with a disproportionate share of the upside potential.[21] It's little wonder some of the employees felt they got a poor deal. The Blue Bell ESOP, also arranged by Kelso & Co., is yet another example of the same situation. This trend continued until, in July 1985, the Labor Department blocked a similar deal at Scott & Fetzer Co., a Cleveland manufacturer. This action set a precedent that stood for two years.

In mid-1987, however, Hospital Corporation of America (HCA) broke this precedent by completing a successful combination of an ESOP buyout and a leveraged management buyout (LMBO). This deal has been the biggest ESOP to date. Despite criticism labeling it as an explicit attempt to create a tax-privileged management buyout, it overcame the stigma of prior two-tiered deals by creating just one class of stock and promising that all classes of owners would be given identical treatment.[22] In this deal, HCA earmarked 104 of its less-profitable hospitals for sale to 25,000 employees. For $1.8 billion, the ESOP received 51 percent of the new company, and the remaining 49 percent to the management group. The chief problem has been that HCA keeps the best hospitals, while the employee-owned company gets smaller, undiversified facilities that account for 35 percent of HCA's current revenues but only 20 percent of profits. The projected cash flow of this new company, furthermore, barely covers the $200 million annual debt-support payments. With hospitals under intense pressure from cost-containment efforts by the insurance industry and the federal government, the company could face problems in the future.

THE DEBATE OVER ESOP FINANCING

Given his firm's unequal treatment of labor and management in several of the ESOPs it arranged, Louis Kelso (the "father" of the ESOP) has very different ideas about reforming the economic order. His expressed aim is "expanding America's ownership base—democratizing its economic power."[23] ESOP financing, in Kelso's vision, is designed to enable people who possess little or no capital to borrow the price of an ownership stake in their employer corporation on the strength of the employer's cash flows. Kelso makes it plain that the heart of this vision is a redistribution of capital in favor of "economic democracy," and that the means for this redistribution is financial leverage combined with tax subsidies. Kelso and his political allies have devised a system of tax preferences that disperse ownership claims to people who might otherwise not be able to accumulate capital as quickly.

In contrast, a more conservative view of economic democracy is concerned with ensuring that owners receive the full benefits of their property rights and that no one is made better off at the cost of another. Kelso's plan expands this view in its aims to accomplish a fundamental redistribution of those property rights, using the taxing authority to convince the reluctant.[24]

Surprisingly, ESOP financing stirs controversy at the other end of the ideological spectrum as well. Some workplace reformers are concerned because nothing in the structure of an ESOP trust requires that labor be given a voice in management. In his *Business Week* column, for example, Robert Kuttner voiced the concern that too often, employee ownership plans do not give workers voting rights and therefore lack a "philosophical commitment to democratize" the workplace.[25] Steven L. Dawson, executive director of the Industrial Cooperative Association (a lobbying organization for employee ownership) reinforced Kuttner's points by arguing that ESOPs give workers a kind of "second-class" ownership: workers get a portion of profits but do not share the control that comes with "first-class" ownership.[26]

The real issue, however, is not employees versus owners or managers versus workers, but rather isolation of any kind from the forces of the marketplace. It is our contention that freedom of the marketplace, more than worker control of the enterprise, is at the heart of economic democracy. Indeed, it seems that difficulties tend to arise if any group gains excessive bargaining power. History is replete, not only with instances of owners taking unfair advantage of workers, but with labor unions, guilds, and management groups entrenching themselves against the forces of the marketplace. Such entrenchment leads to inefficient resource allocation—hence there are fewer goods, higher prices, and a diminished standard of living for everyone.

HOW EXECUTIVE STOCK OWNERSHIP CAN BUILD VALUE

The Value of Organizational Capital

In cutting organizational liabilities the firm's organizational capital may also be impaired or even destroyed completely. Stockholders as well as other stakeholders, therefore, might be better served if the surgery were less radical than is often the case in corporate restructurings. Cornell and Shapiro define organizational capital as the present value of the benefits to be derived from the sale of future implicit claims. Other thinkers have postulated a more complex concept of organizational capital as that of a "lever" to enhance the productivity of pure human capital.

The basic concept of human capital has become widely familiar since its development by Gary Becker and Theodore Schultz. In their view, people are able to acquire skills and knowledge through study, practice, and research, which increase, not only their own productivity, but the income-generating capability of the enterprise in which they work. Pure human capital that is vested in the individual cannot be bought or sold. As a result, there are obvious questions about the extent to which enhancements of human capital can be reflected in the value of equity in a corporation.

Soon after Becker and Schultz introduced the concept of human capital, the role of organizations as systems for harnessing it in ways that amplify the efforts of individuals—that is, levers for pure human capital—began to be considered.[27] Selwyn Becker and Gerald Gordon correspondingly have argued that the formal business organization, even sans its tangible assets, is a tool that is in and of itself a valued form of property.

Prescott and Visscher postulate that such value arises from information concerning both employees' suitability for specific tasks and means to enhance the effectiveness of team efforts. Human capital possessed by individual managers that is firm-specific, however, is perishable—if the individual leaves the employer, the value of his personal firm-specific human capital cannot be transferred to another organization. Thus it is lost completely.

The value of such human capital is enhanced if it is captured in a more lasting form, so that it becomes "organizational capital." In the most recent refinement of the definition, John Tomer describes organizational capital as "human capital in

which the attribute is embodied in the organizational relationships, . . . the organization's repositories of information, or
some combination of the above in order to improve the functioning of the organization [p. 2]."

Tomer's definition makes it clear that organizational capital is
vested in the organization itself, rather than individual employees.
"It is the changed organizational attributes that evoke improved
worker behavior, and thus higher productivity," Tomer continues
to write. "In this pure case, the firm's productivity would be
unchanged should one worker be replaced by another one with
an equal human capital endowment [p. 8]." Unlike an individual's
firm-specific human capital, organizational capital is possessed
by the firm, stored in its information bases, work rules, business
relationships, reputation, culture, and traditions. It is retained by
the organization even after the specific employees who created it
have moved on. A helpful illustration may be found in the small
cadre corps of commissioned and noncommissioned officers who,
during peacetime, maintain military knowledge, skills, and traditions that represent the accumulated heritage of many generations. These officers stand ready to expand their forces quickly
by training and acculturating new recruits in the event of need.
The ability to accomplish this is not vested in any individual, but
instead resides with the group.

Although pure human capital cannot be bought and sold,
organizational capital is independent of any individual and so *can*
be considered a form of property. It is generally not, however,
capable of being isolated precisely enough to be packaged (for
example, in the form of a patent, copyright, or trademark) for
sale or licensing; indeed, the value of organizational capital can
be reflected only through the firm's securities. This difficulty of
definition may even raise questions about whether organizational
capital exists at all. Several sources, however, report a growing
body of evidence that organizational changes can enhance productivity, even without any additional investment in equipment
or other tangible capital.[28]

Furthermore, the huge quantity of effort expended for the sole purpose of maintaining society's array of institutionalized business organizations bears witness to the value they represent. Any organization consumes some amount of effort which serves no direct useful purpose external to the organization. This effort cannot be billed to specific customers and is charged as "overhead" (for example, internal communications and record-keeping). Of course, good management requires a continual effort to control such expenditures, but they cannot be eliminated entirely—and any cost will be tolerated over the long term only if offsetting benefits are perceived. Only the most rugged individualists can honestly dismiss the value of organizations across the board.

Advances in technology are making it possible for the firm to avoid decreases in productivity when retired experts are replaced by those with lesser human capital endowments. Expert system computer programs are being designed to capture the expertise of key individuals, combine it, preserve it, and make it available throughout the organization. Feigenbaum, McCorduck, and Nii therefore formulated the concept of the "expert company" as a repository of information in the form of inter-related expert systems. However, once the reduction of individual expertise to knowledge bases has been accomplished a potential market may develop for its sale or licensing. Then it becomes intellectual property, rather than organizational capital.

Can Organizational Capital Become a Liability?

Although it is natural to think of a firm's organizational capital as having a positive value, it is possible that investors may view the capital's value as negative. In their widely used corporate finance textbook, Brealey and Myers suggest that in some cases, when protection of the organization takes precedence over shareholders' interests, management has a negative net present value. Then the market value of its equity will not reflect the full value of the assets that are recorded in its balance sheet.[29]

A case in point is the situation faced by the oil and gas industry during the mid-eighties. During this time many executives complained that the stock market had seriously undervalued their oil reserves. Indeed, McConnell and Muscarella found an average decrease in stock price due to announcements of increased capital expenditure companies for oil and gas exploration efforts. They concluded that the stock market's response was a vote of no confidence in the firms' prospects and the incumbent management's investment decisions—in their view, stockholders would have preferred to invest the cash themselves in other opportunities.

As a result of this situation the majority of the integrated oil and gas companies underwent one or more forms of restructuring during the eighties. These restructurings included activities designed to reduce management's discretionary control over the firm's cash flows (for example, the sell-off or spinoff of oil and gas reserves into publicly traded limited partnerships and royalty trusts, and the distribution of corporate assets to shareholders via leveraged share repurchases and extraordinary cash dividends). Evidence reviewed in the previous chapter has confirmed that shareholder wealth was enhanced via these actions.

Restructuring to Enhance the Value of Organizational Capital

If the firm can redesign its managerial contracts in ways that better align managerial incentives with those of the owners, the result should be increased value for the firm's organizational capital. Management buyouts represent the purest form of such restructuring. In these arrangements managers and owners become one; thus the incentive-alignment problem evaporates. Other, less-intense forms of ownership incentives have become even more widespread. As revealed in Chapter 4, such restructurings tend to significantly enhance the wealth of shareholders as well as managers.

Threats of takeover or pressure from organized shareholder groups, for example, have forced major U.S. airlines to take evasive actions, such as shedding nonairline operations (for example, hotels, rental car agencies, and catering services). Leasing of aircraft is also becoming widespread; this includes flexible arrangements that allow cancellation of the lease if a change in operations removes the need for the aircraft. In addition to these more mundane restructuring activities, top executives (such as UAL's Stephen Wolf) have received substantial ownership stakes in efforts to align their interests more closely with those of outside stockholders. Ownership of airlines by pilots or other rank-and-file employees is also becoming a strong possibility in the near future.

When boards of directors offer ownership incentives to key executives in an attempt to revitalize a company, they are making an investment in the formation of organizational capital that they hope will pay off in greater wealth for the existing stockholders. Executive ownership gives management strong incentives to break down organizational inefficiencies and seek greater cooperation in the workplace. To the extent that executive ownership increases organizational effectiveness by altering incentives and making management more pro-active, it enhances the cash flows of the firm.

The U.S. Repeating Arms Company (USRAC), which underwent a leveraged buyout in 1984, offers an example. Shortly after the LBO, USRAC reported that orders had increased by 40 percent from the previous year. New products were the key to USRAC's success, supplemented by cuts in staff overhead. More importantly, workers reported that after the LBO, management became more aware of what workers do, resulting in a dramatic increase in productivity.[30] Industrial manufacturer Avondale Industries Inc. (Boston) provides yet another example. It was sold off by previous owner Ogden Corp. in a classic leveraged buyout, with employees and managers getting most of the equity. Cook reports that the company turned itself around through improvements in work practices and product quality, both attributed to the ownership incentives for employees and management.

An even more dramatic turnaround occurred when USX Corp. closed its Geneva Steel operation. Lawyers Joseph and Christopher Cannon, with eight other investors, bought the corporation for $40 million. Since then, they have reversed the aging, inefficient plant, and now it is generating profits of $40 per ton instead of large losses. The Cannons saw potential where former owners saw only aggravation and losses and profited from their vision. Weiner reports that they succeeded by returning to basics, dropping obsolete or marginal products, and introducing new products with higher profit margins. They also instituted a program of continual quality upgrades and improved productivity through continual interaction among owner/managers and workers.

SUMMARY

Too little employee representation in the circle of owners may result in missed opportunities for cost reduction and increased productivity, yet too much may result in slower long-term growth potential for the company. The ideal mix of employee and outside ownership is a delicate balance, which may differ greatly from one enterprise to another. Enterprises that depend heavily upon human capital for their productivity or enterprises that must contend with powerful labor unions stand to gain the most from employee ownership. At the same time, the lowest costs occur in those enterprises with limited potential for future growth.

By encouraging an increased proportion of employee owner-ship across the board, however, the ESOP tax preferences could create mischief in two ways. The tax preferences can sustain a dying enterprise, thus creating an imbalance in the industry. This imbalance holds back stronger competitors and creates economic inefficiency as a result. Perhaps even more damaging in the long run, these preferences may discourage valuable investment in new technologies and other growth opportunities by fostering an overly cautious attitude brought on by inefficient diversification.

The marketplace has shown an ability to find areas where employee ownership is important without the encouragement of tax preferences. Yet some individuals suppose that the marketplace is too slow in making necessary changes and that it needs a boost in the form of tax incentives. The marketplace, however, has time and again proved its remarkable resiliency and adaptability, and the lessons of history suggest that we interfere with its normal functions at our peril. When the benefits of employee ownership exceed its costs, the marketplace can be expected to seek them out on its own.

When multibillion-dollar tax incentives are lavished, however, we are in danger of serious distortions. ESOP financing brings large rewards at the expense of the tax collector, but to one and all it brings a significant change in the way investments in new technology are evaluated and financed. This may in some cases help shareholders wrest control over free cash flows from reluctant management (and so accomplish a much-needed reallocation of resources to higher-valued uses). Yet it may also hold resources longer than necessary in low-valued uses, or it may hamper the growth of an enterprise that would otherwise have higher potential.

Finding a wise balance of employee ownership for a given enterprise is intimately tied in with the problem of allocating the fair share of output to providers of labor and capital. Mature, diversified corporations with strong labor unions and few growth opportunities are the best candidates for ESOP financing. Such companies, however, can be harnessed effectively by other highly leveraged financing arrangements such as LBOs, leveraged recapitalizations, and takeovers. These arrangements also substantially reduce the tax payments made by the company and commit the cash flows to debt support payments.

NOTES

1. U.S. Office of Management and Budget. Reported in *Business Week*, April 15, 1985, p. 94.
2. National Center for Employee Ownership, July 1987.

3. *Wall Street Journal*, October 27, 1987, p. 1.

4. See John Hoerr, "A Company Where Everybody Is the Boss," p. 98.

5. See John Hoerr, Galvin Stevenson, and James Norman, "ESOPs: Revolution or Ripoff?" pp. 94–97, for an estimate of 70 such bailouts.

6. Douglas R. Sease, "ESOPs Weren't Meant to Be Bailouts."

7. For an in-depth analysis, see Eugene Fama and Michael Jensen, "Organizational Forms," pp. 108–18.

8. See, for example, J. Brickley, R. Lease, and Clifford Smith, "Ownership Structure."

9. See A. Marcus, "Risk Sharing."

10. The outside shareholders can diversify away firm-specific risk in their portfolios, whereas the managers cannot.

11. See Michael C. Jensen and W. Meckling, "Theory of the Firm," pp. 305–60, for the classic theoretical analysis of the concept of "agency cost."

12. See Stewart Myers, "Determinants of Corporate Borrowing," pp. 147–75.

13. Even if the ESOP held only a portion of the stock, there would still be a strong incentive to pay out all earnings. Suppose, for example, the ESOP owned 50 percent of the stock in the employer corporation. Then, half of every dollar paid in dividends would be deductible, whereas all of a dollar retained would be taxed. If the corporation earned $10 million, it could pay out as much as $8.3 million in dividends at one extreme (100 percent payout) or retain $6.6 million for reinvestment at the other extreme (100 percent retention). Starting from so far behind, the corporation would need a significant advantage to be able to reinvest its earnings more profitably than what the stockholders could do on their own.

14. The "free cash flow" of a firm is the excess of funds over what is required to finance the economically sound expansion projects available to the firm.

15. This idea was first developed in Michael C. Jensen, "Agency Costs of Free Cash Flow," pp. 305–60.

16. *The Dallas Morning News*, "Firms Find New Role."

17. See Judith Valente and Scott Kilman "Pilots May Seek Partner," p. 6; James Ellis and Chuck Hawkins, "The Unraveling of an Idea," pp. 42–43, and Kenneth Labich, "How Dick Ferris Blew It," pp. 42–46, for more details.

18. Quoted in Robert L. Rose, "United Pilots Leader," p. 21.

19. The ESOP acquired 70 percent of the company with a $110 million investment in Class A common stock at a price of $22.50 per share. A group consisting of a Kelso investment fund, plus 26 members of top management, paid $4.3 million for 30 percent of the company, mostly in the form of Class B common stock valued at $2.06 per share. Since the buyout there is no

longer any market in the stock, so a periodic valuation will be made by an independent appraiser. According to the rules, the Class A stock will always be worth about $22 per share more than the Class B stock, but the disparity in the initial values gives management a disproportionate share of the upside. If Class A stock rose to $26, for instance, Class B stock would rise to about $4, representing a 100 percent gain for Class B stock compared to only 16 percent gain for Class A stock.

20. See Pete Engardio, "At Dan River," p. 97.

21. A group of Kelso & Co. investors and 28 Raymond managers paid $5.4 million in cash, stock, and stock options for Class B common stock at $1.09 per share. The ESOP borrowed $100 million in order to buy Class A common stock at $10 per share. The Class B stock, pegged at a price $10 below Class A stock, gives management a disproportionate share of the upside potential. For example, if Class A stock went up 50 percent to $15, then Class B stock would increase nearly fivefold.

22. Gary Weiss, "HCA May Breathe," p. 94.

23. Louis O. and Patricia M. Kelso, *Democracy and Economic Power*, p. xi.

24. After all, the taxpayers get the bill for the "gift" of employee ownership.

25. See, for example, Robert Kuttner, "Worker Ownership," p. 16.

26. See "Letters to the Editor."

27. Harvey Liebenstein, *General X-Efficiency Theory*, and "The Prisoner's Dilemma," pp. 92–97, formalizes the value of the organization in the concept of "X-efficiency" and its opposite "X-inefficiency." The degree of X-inefficiency is defined as "the degree to which actual output is less than maximum output (for given inputs) [*General X-Efficiency Theory*, p. 95]." In Leibenstein's analysis, self-interested individuals taking into account organizational incentives tend to exert less effort than would be optimal from the stockholders' point of view. Since the stock market can be expected to reflect improvements in the organization that increase X-efficiency, such enhancements are indeed translated into marketable capital. Michael C. Jensen and W. Meckling, "Rights and Production Functions," utilize a production function which incorporates a "generalized index describing the range of choice of 'organizational forms' or internal rules of the game available to the firm." In their analysis, this variable plays "an important role in motivating self-interested and maximizing individuals to achieve the physically possible output." Furthermore, A. Alchian and H. Demsetz, "Production, Information Costs," pp. 777–95, hold that the productivity of a team may be greater than the sum of the separate contributions of its individual members.

28. See K. Bradley and A. Gelb, *Worker Capitalism*; Michael Conte and Arnold Tannenbaum, "Employee-Owned Companies," pp. 23–28; A.

Coughlin and R. Schmidt, "Executive Compensation"; Michael C. Jensen and W. Meckling, "Rights and Production Functions," pp. 496–506; D. Kruse, *Employee Ownership*; National Center for Employee Ownership, *Employee Ownership Research Review*; C. Rosen, K. Klein, and K. Young, *Employee Ownership in America*; Jan Svejnar, "Codetermination and Productivity"; Henk Thomas, "The Performance of the Mondragon"; and Daniel Zwerdling, *Workplace Democracy*.

29. Alternatively, a firm's organizational capital may have a positive value, but be eclipsed when a higher value is assessed for its organizational liabilities.

30. Source: "After Leveraged Buyouts," pp. 65–70.

REFERENCES

"After Leveraged Buyouts: Two Companies' Divergent Paths," *Business Week*, February 27, 1984, pp. 65–70.

Alchian, A., and H. Demsetz. "Production, Information Costs, and Economic Organization," *American Economic Review* 62 (December 1972), pp. 777–95.

"Are ESOPs Without Worker Control a Sham?" (letters to editor) *Business Week*, August 3, 1987, p. 6.

Becker, Gary. "Investment in Human Capital: A Theoretical Analysis," *Journal of Political Economy* 50 (October Supplement, 1962), pp. 9–49.

Becker, Selwyn, and Gerald Gordon. "An Entrepreneurial Theory of Formal Organizations," *Administrative Science Quarterly* 11 (December 1966), pp. 315–44.

Bradley, K., and A. Gelb. *Worker Capitalism: The New Industrial Relations* (Cambridge, MA: MIT Press, 1983).

Brealey, Richard A., and Stewart C. Myers. *Principles of Corporate Finance*, 3rd ed. (New York: McGraw-Hill Book Company, 1988).

Brickley, J., R. Lease, and Clifford Smith. "Ownership Structure and Voting on Antitakeover Amendments," *Journal of Financial Economics*, 20 January 1988, pp. 267–291.

Conte, Michael, and Arnold Tannenbaum. "Employee-Owned Companies: Is the Difference Measurable?" *Monthly Labor Review* 10 (July 1978), pp. 23–28.

Cook, James. "The Ownership Culture," *Forbes* 138 (October 6, 1986), p. 72.

Cornell, Bradford, and Alan Shapiro. "Corporate Stakeholders and Corporate Finance," *Financial Management* 16 (Spring 1987), pp. 5–14.

Coughlin, A., and R. Schmidt. "Executive Compensation, Management Turnover, and Firm Performance: An Empirical Investigation," *Journal of Accounting and Economics* 7 (1985).

Ellis, James, and Chuck Hawkins. "The Unraveling of an Idea," *Business Week*, June 22, 1987.

Engardio, Pete. "At Dan River, 'A Lot of Us Feel That We Got Took,' " *Business Week*, April 15, 1985.

Fama, Eugene, and Michael Jensen. "Organizational Forms and Investment Decisions," *Journal of Financial Economics* 14 (June 1985), pp. 108-18.

Feigenbaum, E., P. McCorduck, and H. Nii. *The Rise of the Expert Company* (New York: Times Books, 1988).

"Firms Find New Role for Stock Plans," *The Dallas Morning News*, January 13, 1985.

Hoerr, John. "A Company Where Everybody Is the Boss," *Business Week*, April 15, 1985, p. 98.

Hoerr, John, Gelvin Stevenson, and James Norman. "ESOPs: Revolution or Ripoff?" *Business Week*, April 15, 1985, pp. 94–97.

Jensen, Michael C. "Agency Costs of Free Cash Flow, Corporate Finance and Takeovers," *American Economic Review* (May 1986).

Jensen, Michael C., and W. Meckling. "Theory of the Firm, Managerial Behavior, Agency Costs and Ownership Structure," *Journal of Financial Economics* 3 (1976), pp. 305-60.

Jensen, Michael C., and W. Meckling. "Rights and Production Functions: An Application to Labor-managed Firms and Codetermination," *Journal of Business* 52 (October 1979), pp. 496–506.

Kelso, Louis O. and Patricia H. *Democracy and Economic Power* (Cambridge, MA.: Ballinger Publishing Company, 1986).

Kruse, D. *Employee Ownership and Employee Attitudes: Two Case Studies*, Worker Ownership and Participation Book Series, Vol. 1, Josef Blasi, ed. (Norwood, PA: Norwood Editions, 1984).

Kuttner, Robert. "Worker Ownership: A Commitment That's More Often a Con," *Business Week*, July 6, 1987.

Labich, Kenneth. "How Dick Ferris Blew It," *Fortune*, July 6, 1987.

Liebenstein, Harvey. *General X-Efficiency Theory and Economic Development* (New York: Oxford University Press, 1978).

Liebenstein, Harvey. "The Prisoner's Dilemma in the Invisible Hand: An Analysis of Intrafirm Productivity," *American Economic Review* 71 (May 1982), pp. 92–97.

Marcus, A. "Risk Sharing and the Theory of the Firm," *Bell Journal of Economics* 13 (1982).

McConnell, John, and Chris Muscarella. "Corporate Capital Expenditure Decisions and the Market Value of the Firm," *Journal of Financial Economics* (September 1985), pp. 399–422.

Myers, Stewart. "Determinants of Corporate Borrowing," *Journal of Financial Economics* 5 (1977), pp. 147–75.

National Center for Employee Ownership. *Employee Ownership: Research Review* (Arlington, VA: National Center for Employee Ownership, 1985).

"PAYSOP PLANS for Employee Stock Ownership," *Wall Street Journal*, October 27, 1987, p. 1.

Prescott, E., and M. Visscher. "Organizational Capital," *Journal of Political Economy* 88 (June 1980), pp. 446–81.

Rose, Robert L. "United Pilots Leader Stays on Course," *Wall Street Journal*, July 17, 1987.

Rosen, C., K. Klein, and K. Young. *Employee Ownership in America: the Equity Solution* (Lexington, MA: Lexington Books, 1986).

Schultz, Theodore. *Investment in Human Capital: The Role of Education and of Research* (New York: Free Press, 1971).

Sease, Douglas R. "ESOPs Weren't Meant to Be Bailouts," *Wall Street Journal*, December 2, 1985.

Svejnar, Jan. "Codetermination and Productivity: Empirical Evidence from the Federal Republic of Germany," in Derek C. Jones and Jan Svejnar, eds., *Participatory and Self-Managed Firms* (Lexington, MA: Lexington Books, 1982).

Thomas, Henk. "The Performance of the Mondragon Cooperatives in Spain," in Derek C. Jones and Jan Svejnar, eds., *Participatory and Self-Managed Firms* (Lexington, MA: Lexington Books, 1982).

Tomer, John. *Organizational Capital* (New York: Praeger Publishers, 1987).

Valente, Judith, and Scott Kilman. "Pilots May Seek Partner to Buy Parent of United," *Wall Street Journal*, April 27, 1987.

Wall Street Journal, October 27, 1987, p. 1.

Weiner, Steve. "Making Hay from Nuts and Bolts," *Forbes* 141 (May 2, 1988), pp. 72–76.

Weiss, Gary. "HCA May Breathe New Life into ESOPs," *Business Week*, June 15, 1987.

Zwerdling, Daniel. *Workplace Democracy: A Guide to Workplace Ownership, Participation, and Self-Management Experiments in the United States and Europe* (New York: Harper Colophon Books, 1980).

Government Documents

Deficit Reduction Act of 1984
Economic Recovery Tax Act of 1981
Employee Retirement Income Security Act (ERISA) of 1974
Internal Revenue Code, Section 415, paragraph 19,566
Tax Code, Sections 542 and 543; also Section 44G, paragraph 4281
Tax Reduction Act of 1975
Tax Reform Act of 1986

Chapter 6

Project Financing: Limited-Recourse Debt with a Significant Equity Component

In a project financing an individual venture stands alone as an independent entity, and its nature is such that it has a clearly defined lifespan. Cash flows are paid out to the owners as they are earned—rather than reinvested in new projects under the same management—and the legal entity set up to establish the project has a finite life. There need not be any debt involved in such an arrangement (for example, many R&D limited partnerships are all-equity, but are clearly finite-lived, project-oriented entities). When there is debt, however, the creditors have recourse only to the assets and cash flows of the project itself, without further recourse to the owners. The use of debt in a project financing is thus comparable to the issuance of revenue bonds by a municipality, with payments restricted to the proceeds from a particular set of user fees or tax revenues,[1] and a project's viability as an independent financial entity likewise depends upon the substance behind the projected revenue stream.

Limited-recourse debt is another example of "debt" that has a significant equity component for investors—imposing debtlike restrictions on corporate management. Because investors have recourse only to the cash flows of a specific set of activities involving a subset of the assets under corporate management, such debt offers management some of the flexibility *inherent* in equity financing. The requirement to pay out most of the project's cash flow as interest, however, conveys to investors the tax advantages of debt along with explicit control over the decision of how to reinvest the cash flows.

Far from being a johnny-come-lately gimmick that has yet to stand the test of time, venture-by-venture financing of finite-lived projects has ancient roots, and was the rule in commerce until the nineteenth century.[2] Project financing did not die with the industrial revolution but continued to be used through the years by European financiers for separately accountable ventures, such as overseas mineral exploration projects. In the continual experimentation to discover more effective ways to organize economic ventures, it is becoming increasingly common for corporations to establish individual projects as separate, finite-lived entities.[3] Project financing is being used extensively, not only to fund real estate development and oil and gas exploration, but independent electric power generation facilities, factories, and research and development efforts. Yet there has been little analysis of project financing in the academic literature, and even the descriptive material that is available is sparse and sometimes contradictory. Nonetheless, during the 1980s a vigorous market in the private placement of limited-recourse project financing has confronted financial managers in several industries with the decision of whether to make project financing arrangements or raise the funds for a project on the parent's own account.[4]

A problem for academics is that there are no ready-made data bases on project financing, and not even a consistent description of the practice in the published literature. Shah and Thakor provide the only mathematic-theoretical analysis of the rationale for project financing in print to date. Their theory is built upon the premise that project financing is used for very large, high-risk projects, but this premise is drawn from only two cases (their primary example is a proposed tunnel beneath the English Channel). We have gathered data on a large number of project financings in order to overcome this difficulty.

Our analysis reveals that project financing is commonly used for relatively modest-size, low-risk projects.[5] A long list of

Fortune 500 companies (such as du Pont, Scott Paper, Union Carbide, and Sun Oil, to name a few) have chosen project financing over internal financing for electrical generation facilities constructed at their plants, refineries, and enhanced oil recovery units. In fact, project financing has become the dominant practice in the rapidly growing independent (non-utility) power production industry.[6] The overwhelming dominance of a particular form of financing for a whole class of capital investment projects indicates that the nature of these ventures makes project financing the most attractive alternative. The common thread among the project financings we have observed is that each one reflects a community of interests among a group of independent entities.

Thus, project financing offers a finite-lived alternative to merger. Selecting project financing versus internal financing is a more radical choice than most financial decisions, however, because it involves an alternative organizational form that is fundamentally different from the traditional corporation in two significant ways that have implications for the reorganization of business activities: (1) the legal entity that gives the project substance is finite-lived, with its identity defined by that specific project; and (2) as a result, the cash flows generated by the project (including depreciation/depletion) are paid directly to the investors, who make the reinvestment decisions themselves. Unlike the traditional integrated corporation, management does not have the "first option" in deciding how to reinvest the project's cash flows.

BACKGROUND INFORMATION ON PROJECT FINANCING

Organizational Forms Used in Project Financing

When there is a single corporate sponsor, a project financing can be arranged simply by negotiating nonrecourse loans through special-purpose subsidiaries or trusts. Other project financing arrangements are structured around nonrecourse leveraged leases, in which the lease obligations are payable solely from the assets and cash flows of the project. In the case of joint ventures, the simplest form for a project financing is a general partnership among the parties in the venture. A partnership formed to develop a specific oil field and then be dissolved when the properties are sold or depleted, for example, might qualify. The key criterion is that creditors be willing to make contracts with no recourse beyond the assets and cash flows of the partnership.

When some of the partners in a joint venture wish to forego active management involvement in the technical matters of day-to-day operations (or when a single sponsor wants to raise outside equity capital), a limited partnership can be used.[7] Because the debt is nonrecourse, even general partners enjoy limited liability with respect to the project's debt; but in order to contain potential liabilities arising from other types of claims, the parent companies often form separately incorporated subsidiaries to serve as general partner in their stead.[8]

A British Petroleum Venture Offers an Example of How Limited-Recourse Debt Works like Equity, but with Stiffer Rules

British Petroleum's $945 million project financing for the development of its North Sea oil field (the Forties Field) in 1972, arranged through a syndicate of 66 banks, offers useful details of how such a venture can be structured.[9] At the time, it was the largest industrial loan in history. The basic terms of the arrangement dictated that the lenders had recourse only to the assets of the project in the event of default, so the other assets of British Petroleum were protected from the consequences of project failure.

This was achieved by creating a new entity, Norex, which was controlled by the banks. The loan was made to Norex, and Norex paid the proceeds to BP Development (a subsidiary of British Petroleum) in return for contracts for the future delivery of oil from the Forties Field.[10] Norex in turn contracted to sell the oil to BP Trading Company. With the funds from the sale of the oil, Norex would make debt service payments to the banks.[11]

The banks were protected by contracts with BP Development, describing all of the development steps in detail, and compliance with the plan was guaranteed by British Petroleum. The risk taken by the banks was that the amount of oil available from the field would not be sufficient to repay the loans.

PROJECT FINANCING FOR RESEARCH AND DEVELOPMENT

Sec. 174 [which allows immediate deduction of research and experimentation expenditures as a business expense] was enacted to encourage the search for new products by both established and upcoming businesses.
 —U.S. Supreme Court, in the case of *Snow v. Commissioner*[12]

Prior to the U.S. Supreme Court's 1974 decision in *Snow v. Commissioner*, research and experimentation expenses arising from efforts to develop a new product or technology could be deducted only if the taxpayer were *already engaged* in a related trade or business. A company conducting research as the first step toward entry into an industry or product line was denied the advantage of the research deduction—the new entrant would have to wait until it could carry the losses forward into future years. This of course meant that the tax benefits arising from the research and experimentation deduction had a lower present value for a new entrant (which was forced to defer them) than for an established company (which could take advantage of them earlier). The *Snow* decision extended the advantage of immediate deductibility to taxpayers who simply have a *legitimate intent* to enter into a trade or business related to the research effort. The court's decision thus had the effect of putting new entrants on a "level playing field" with established companies.

As meaningful as it was, this action failed to extend the level playing field to startup companies. A startup corporation would face much higher research costs than an established corporation because a startup has no income against which to deduct expenses, while an established corporation could make immediate use of the research deduction. Although creating a level playing field was the court's explicit intention, it took innovative financiers to extend the benefits to startups. These innovators realized that *Snow v. Commissioner* laid the foundation for the limited partners in a specialized R&D partnership to fully utilize the deduction and pass some of the advantages on to the sponsoring corporation.

RDLPs are limited partnerships formed for the purpose of conducting research and developing new products or processes. The limited partners have no involvement in day-to-day management decisions and have limited liability in the enterprise; but the general partner who manages the affairs of the partnership has unlimited liability for its obligations. RDLPs typically own no physical assets whatsoever—only intellectual property, such as patents, formulae, or data. All of their work is done by contractors, so they function as a means of defining relationships among providers of resources, rather than as entities that actually perform work. The partnership itself pays no taxes, but all income or loss is divided among the partners and consolidated with their other earnings for tax purposes.

Most of the existing RDLPs are pure equity in the sense that all funds come from the sale of limited partnership units or from capital invested by the general partners. The rules governing the distribution of cash flows, however, qualify these arrangements as dequity financings. The limited partners are assured that they will receive all or most of the project's cash flows until they have received an agreed-upon total. Only then will the general partners begin receiving a significant proportion. For example, one such RDLP agreement provided that the limited partners would receive all of the cash flows from royalties until they had received their initial investment. Then they would receive 90 percent of the cash flows until they received a total amount equal to twice their investment. After that, cash flows would be divided equally between the general partner and the limited partners.

The first RDLP in the records of the U.S. Department of Commerce was formed in 1978 when John Delorean raised $20 million to develop his ill-fated sports car. Since that perhaps inglorious beginning, RDLPs have proliferated rapidly. They now range in size from a few million dollars to a hundred million, and by the end of 1985 they had been used to raise a total of more than $3.4 billion. For comparison, the total combined R&D spending in fiscal 1983–84 for du Pont, Eastman Kodak, Digital Equipment, Hewlett-Packard, and Xerox added up to just under $3.5 billion.

The Tax Reform Act of 1986, however, eliminated the ability to deduct the limited partners' share of R&D expenses against other income, such as salary, interest, dividends, and active business income. Expenses arising from passive investments such as limited partnerships can be charged only against income from passive investments.[13] Income and losses from limited partnerships are generally considered to be passive. The definition of passive activities in the tax reform legislation (p. H7634) specifically includes limited partnerships that generate deductions allowable under Sec. 174 (research and experimentation expenses), leaving no doubt that deductions arising from a limited partner's interest in an RDLP are to be treated as passive. The losses must be carried forward, unless the taxpayer has sufficient current income from other passive investments against which to offset them (or past passive investment income in the carryback period). As one might suspect, though, there are ways to utilize passive losses. In some cases it is possible for RDLP losses to be deducted from active business income within a closely held corporation. Furthermore, there are over 30 publicly traded master limited partnerships representing claims to the cash flows from over $10 billion worth of assets,[14] with more in the offing, and a large number of "plain vanilla" passive investments that are producing cash flows. These funds also represent potential fuel for postreform RDLP financings. In the latest parlance of Wall Street, RDLPs create "PALs" (passive accounting losses) for cash-rich "PIGs" (passive income generators), thus making the PIGs more valuable to their owners. A lonely PIG subjects its owner to higher taxes. A PIG with the right circle of PALs, however, can produce tax-free income; and the PALs will hopefully turn into PIGs themselves one day.

Ironically, the new tax law unbalances the level playing field, giving noncorporate upstarts (that is, proprietorships, partnerships, and S-corporations) an advantage over any corporation. When the upstart is an entity that is not taxed as a corporation, the project's cash flows are taxed only once, at the individual rate. Now that the individual rate is below the corporate rate, the tax liabilities of the noncorporate upstart are clearly less than those of any corporation, given the same pretax cash flows.

Since 1983 the trend in R&D project financing has been toward project pools managed by R&D subsidiaries of investment banking firms and often funded by institutional investors (Merrill Lynch, Prudential-Bache, E. F. Hutton, and Morgan Stanley have formed R&D management subsidiaries). Such direct involvement in fundamental business ventures by financial institutions is a departure from modern tradition and stimulates formidable competition from new entrants.

The Early History of Project Financing

An arrangement that enabled medieval Italian bankers to undertake a mining venture in England offers a 700-year-old example with several parallels to the British Petroleum North Sea project. Through it, the English Crown negotiated a loan from the Frescobaldi (a leading Florentine merchant-banking firm) with payment to be made from the output of the Devon silver mines. The arrangement was crystallized in the form of a lease for the total output of the mines during the year 1299.[15] The contract entitled the Italian venturers to control the operation of the mines for one year and take as much unrefined ore as they could extract, paying all costs of operation. No guarantees were made, however, concerning the total amount of ore that could be mined or the value of refined metal extracted from the ore. Thus, the risks faced by these long-ago bankers were much like those faced by their modern-day counterparts in the North Sea venture.[16]

Project Financing Was the Rule Until Intercontinental Commerce Became a Continuous Process

Until the seventeenth century, moreover, the rule in commerce was to finance trading expeditions on a voyage-by-voyage basis. That is, cargoes and ships were liquidated and the profits divided among the investors at the conclusion of each voyage. New investors then had to be found to back the next one. Although many investors willingly "rolled over" their money, they did so at their own discretion. To better understand the implications of the modern resurgence of project financing, it is helpful to take a brief look into history to see why project financing went into the background in the first place.

With the consolidation of political power at the end of the Middle Ages, companies of merchants sought privileges in the form of preferential customs duties and outright monopolies— which were not granted to individuals, but only to chartered trading companies.[17] At first, these were regulated companies of "mere merchants" (a credential that could be earned only by serving an apprenticeship abroad) who raised money among themselves in the traditional manner on a voyage-by-voyage basis. Rapid growth, however, levied mounting capital requirements, which could be met only by expanding the base of investors to the broader public.

The means for doing this was found in the joint-stock companies, the forerunners of the modern corporation, which could draw capital from anyone willing to risk it. Although this ability was not entirely new—it was an extension of the long-time practice of merchants taking deposits, either for interest or for a share of profits (which made them merchant-bankers)— formalizing the practice through the sale of stock allowed it to be expanded to a larger scale.[18]   Unlike a modern corporation, though, the early companies were committed to allowing the funds invested with them to be withdrawn directly from the treasury, analogous to an open-end mutual fund. To meet redemption demands, however, a company might be forced to liquidate inventories, or other assets, which in the extreme could lead to ruin. To ensure a regular flow of trade, the companies found that they needed permanent capital, and this led to a revolutionary change in business organization.

Although the Dutch East India Company began operations under a charter which authorized members to withdraw their capital at will, it suspended such repayments in 1612. Its rival, the British East India Company, also restricted such payments the same year. Apparently this was not an easy transition for the British company, though, because for the next half-century it vacillated between the traditional practice of settling accounts at the end of each voyage and the newer practice of carrying forward the balances to later voyages.

The reason both companies moved toward impounding permanent capital is readily understandable. Their funds were tied up in warehouse buildings and land, much of it half a world away from home, as well as great fleets, and the values could not be readily realized in the thin markets of the day. The situation owed significantly to changes in shipbuilding, the "high technology" of the era, as well as to the voyages of discovery. Over the last half of the sixteenth century, the carrying power of merchant fleets increased dramatically, transforming intercontinental ocean commerce from a series of independent ventures into a process involving a steady flow of goods. An independent captain could not simply sail into an Asian port and expect to load a cargo from the dockside markets at reasonable prices. Permanent representatives (factors) and warehouses (called "factories") had to be stationed at the foreign ports, and treaties negotiated to protect them.

The sunk costs required the companies to carry a burden of what they referred to at the time as "dead stock." Not only was it illiquid, it was also next to impossible to allocate fairly to the accounts of individual voyages. Liquidity for this dead stock came to be provided in the secondary markets in place of on-demand redemption.[19] Trading in the stock of the chartered companies joined the commodity-trading, foreign exchange, and insurance-brokering activities in the merchant's exchanges that formed the hub of commerce in the major trading cities.[20]

THEORY OF PROJECT FINANCING

James Mao points out that in order for projects to gain limited-recourse financing as independent entities, the relationships among the participants must be spelled out in detailed contracts. Since no responsible lender would enter a truly nonrecourse lending arrangement with a thinly capitalized project entity, the situation can be more correctly described as limited-recourse financing. Worenklein addresses the project's requirement for independent substance in terms of "sources of credit support" in the form of contracts to purchase output from the project or supply necessary inputs at controlled cost. Even though the project's sponsors do not provide an outright guarantee of the project's credit-worthiness, they provide credit support through such contractual obligations.

Because of the need for independent substance, project financing arrangements invariably involve deep relationships among two or more independent entities. Project financing can work only in situations that allow such relationships to be established and maintained at a supportable cost. The creditors are protected if the project should perform poorly as a result of one of the participants welshing on its part of the agreement and bear only the risk of some failure that might be caused by factors outside the bounds of the contractual protection. Because the creditors can sue the project entity, which in turn can sue the defaulting party, the pockets of the project are as deep as those of the participants (at least with regard to contractual obligations such as the purchase of inputs or the sale of output).

Sarmet even takes the concept of independent substance to a noncontractual level, by invoking the need for a genuine "community of interest" among the parties who sponsor the project. Only if it is in their best interests for the project to succeed, he argues, will they do all they can to make sure that it does. Indeed, for experienced practitioners the acid test of soundness for such ventures is whether all parties (including project lenders) have something to gain from the arrangement. In order to understand project financing arrangements, therefore, one must find reasons for each of the parties to gain; and it is therefore unlikely that any single rationale will fully explain the phenomenon of project financing.

Convenience Value for Participants in Project Financing Arrangements

Tax Advantages of Project Financing. Project financing is part of a larger trend toward increasing direct investment by individuals and institutions. In the current tax environment the traditional corporation often is not the optimal form of organization for entities whose primary function is to own natural resources and capital equipment—the tax differential for partnerships and trusts continues to give them a potential advantage in such "caretaker" activities. It is clearly undesirable for a tax-sheltered pension fund, tax-exempt endowment fund, or foreign investor to own real estate or capital equipment indirectly via stock in a tax-paying corporation, so long as it is possible to create arrangements that pass income untaxed directly to investors.[21] For individuals as well, direct investment via limited partnership or trust arrangements offers the advantage of avoiding the double taxation to which corporate dividends are exposed.[22]

The primary problem for an institutional investor in a direct investment, moreover, is to avoid being considered as an active participant in the business activity, which could expose it to taxation as a corporation. If a limited partnership or trust arrangement should prove ineffective, an alternative is a leveraged lease arrangement in which a financial entrepreneur takes the equity stake and borrows most of the cost of the equipment from the institution, with the cash flows from the lease agreement satisfying the requirement for independent substance in terms of sources of credit support. When the lender's recourse is limited to the cash flows from the lease and the lessee has substantial freedom of cancellation, the institutional lender's risk/reward profile is very much the same as if it owned the asset directly. Tax liabilities arising from the cash flows through the lease are substantially reduced when the lessee deducts lease payments, the entrepreneur deducts interest expense, and the institutional investor is exempt from taxation of interest earnings.

Project Financing Bonds Cash Flows. The common advantage for investors in all forms of project financing is that the entity created in a project financing has a finite life, and the "dividend policy" of the project is spelled out in writing. Thus investors have control over decisions about reinvesting the cash flows, resolving potential conflicts of interest that arise when management has discretion over reinvestment.

Investors may have reason to doubt whether managers will be sufficiently demanding when comparing investment opportunities within the corporation to the alternatives available outside. Moreover, there have always been doubts about the utility to an investor of a sum of money placed for a long term at the discretion of a company over which he has little influence, and Jensen formalized them in the concept of the "agency cost of free cash flow." As Williamson argues, furthermore, project financing should be value-enhancing for ventures that lend themselves to governance by rules and contracts, as opposed to the discretion of management. When the environment is stable, the argument goes, management discretion adds to investors' uncertainty without contributing substantial cost reduction.[23]

Project financing has the power to be a catalyst for change in the governance of business activities. Generally, when a corporation chooses to undertake an investment project, cash flows from existing activities fund the newcomer; and management has the option to roll over the project's capital into still newer ventures within the company later on—without submitting them to the discipline of the capital market. This option gives corporate management considerable power, which has been a focal point in the debate over shareholder rights. With project financing, in contrast, the assets and cash flows associated with each project are accounted for separately. Funding for the new project is negotiated from outside sources, and as the project runs its course, the capital is returned to the investors, who decide for themselves how to reinvest it. By returning such decisions to the marketplace, project financing accomplishes a fundamental reform.

It can be argued, however, that managers should exercise reinvestment discretion when they are better informed than investors. When the assets under management are natural resources, generic production facilities, real estate, or some other category that requires little more than caretaker management, however, such an argument is hard to support. Then it can be argued instead that stockholders have reason for increased uncertainty as a result of management discretion over reinvestment decisions. Cornell and Shapiro point out that managers not only have interests of their own that are at variance with those of the stockholders but also must satisfy other "stakeholders" whose interests often conflict with those of the stockholders.[24]

Regulatory and Legal Advantages of Project Financing. Project financing may offer economies of scale in controlling regulatory and legal costs for the owner of the host site. A chemical company or an oil company that undertakes an electric power cogeneration[25] project on its own, for example, faces substantial management costs in an activity involving unfamiliar technologies, laws, and regulatory bodies. As Hu points out, however, from the viewpoint of the specialized general contractor, however, a typical cogeneration project represents a standardized undertaking in which experience and relationships gained from other projects are readily applicable to the project at hand. The economic viability of the project, furthermore, depends upon continued cooperation with several outside organizations over which the owner of the host site has no direct control (that is, the utility that agrees to buy the electricity and the company that has agreed to supply fuel), and the possibility of one day having to enforce such agreements adds another potential management cost for the owner of the host site. The specialists' continuing attention to such matters over the life of the project is heightened when the developer has an equity stake as general partner in the project. The project's independent status and the developer's willingness to make a long-term commitment to it thus resolve risks that the owner of the host site would face if it financed the project internally.[26]

When the lead player in a joint venture is relatively stronger than the other parties, it would prefer that all parties enter into contracts with an independent project entity—as opposed to the alternative of letting the others enter into contracts directly with the leader. In a cogeneration project located in a densely industrialized area, for example, several neighboring chemical plants or refineries might agree to buy steam from the facility, while the local utility contracts to buy electric power. If the lead player in the venture were the focal point of the contracting, it could be left with increased obligations in the event one of the weaker parties ceased to buy steam—the leader would still have the obligation to supply the agreed-upon amount of generating capacity to the utility but would have a diminished outlet for the sale of steam. With the contracts focused on an independent entity, however, such problems would be forestalled—in this case, the leader would face only its own obligation to buy steam from the facility.

Finally, project financing arrangements overcome regulatory barriers for banks which desire an equity stake in a venture. Banks are generally prevented from owning more than 5 percent of the equity in a nonfinancial business, but the allowable proportion increases to as much as 50 percent if the bank exercises no control over the enterprise.[27] First of all, it can be argued that making a loan to an entity with limited recourse to its sponsors is indistinguishable from taking an equity stake in the project. Furthermore, a project financing arranged as a limited partnership allows a substantial nonvoting equity stake, while still contractually binding the cash flows from the venture. Likewise, a project financing in the form of a nonrecourse lease allows a bank to take a substantial equity stake in a project without running afoul of the limits upon nonfinancial business activities. The practice of establishing separate legal entities for projects also allows several banks to share in taking equity positions in a pool of projects, while still conforming to the regulatory limits.

Project Financing Privatizes Bankruptcy. The legal situation has another dimension as well, which makes it possible for project financing to enhance the operational flexibility of machines that not only are capable of operating with relatively little direct labor input but also are readily redeployable to alternate uses. The bulk of their costs are incurred up front, and their economic viability depends, not only upon maintaining a positive spread between the cost of input and the price of output, but maintaining the capability of relocating quickly if the host site goes out of business. When the output is generic (such as beverage cans which may be sold to any proprietary bottler) maintaining a market is facilitated by remaining free from the fortunes of any particular brandname. Independent ownership makes it easier to find outlets to absorb the full capacity of the plant.

If one of the parties defaults on its obligations, furthermore, it can be easier for secured creditors to redeploy assets to alternative uses if they are owned by a joint venture that is organized independently. The time involved in resolving a bankruptcy increases with the number of potential claimants and the complexity of their claims. Over the years, a mature corporation accumulates a large burden of claims against it, including pension obligations, which must be adjudicated fairly. An independent joint venture to build an automated plant, in contrast, has a light burden of such claims. The process of bankruptcy, therefore, can be streamlined by means of project financing. Without invoking too much poetic license, it might even be said that the use of project financing puts "legal wheels" on assets that already possess a high degree of inherent mobility.

Project Financing Makes the Capital Market More Complete and Enhances Incentives for Key People. Another potentially significant nontax benefit is that project financing makes the capital markets more complete by providing investors with a "pure play" that was not previously available. Without R&D limited partnerships, for example, an investor wishing to participate in a firm's research and development efforts would have to buy stock in the whole company, which is analogous to someone who wants a steak being forced to buy a whole steer. It can be argued that investors are willing to pay a premium in order to get the specific thing they want. In a project financing, furthermore, the investment is subjected to outside scrutiny before being undertaken. The investors, that is, have a direct say in the capital investment decision, thus enhancing the efficiency of resource allocation.

Project financing can enhance incentives for key employees, too, by enabling them to take a direct ownership stake in the operations under their control.[28] The key players in the Merrill Lynch R&D Management Company, for example, are among the general partners in the R&D partnerships they manage. They are therefore strongly motivated to select the most promising projects and do all that is within their power to facilitate successful outcomes.

The Informational Asymmetry Arguments

Project-Specific Informational Asymmetry. Shah and Thakor argue that project financing reduces the costs of informational asymmetry associated with large-scale, high-risk projects. The essence of this concept is that managers often possess valuable information about new projects that cannot be communicated unambiguously to the capital market. One barrier to communication is the cost to the company of providing extensive technical information, as well as the cost to the investor of processing it.[29]

Another potential barrier to communication is the need to keep competitors in the dark in order to maintain a competitive advantage. When managers have information that is not publicly available, however, raising funds for new investment opportunities may be costly unless proprietary information of value to competitors is revealed to the public. Here again, project financing provides a potential resolution. Financing a research and development project through a privately placed project financing, for example, can solve the problem. By revealing the necessary information about the project to a small group of investors, the company can obtain a fair price for the financing without revealing the proprietary information to the public. Since the investors in the project have a stake in maintaining confidentiality, the danger of an information leak is small.

This reasoning is logically consistent with the premise that project financing is used for projects which are not "transparent," that is, which impose high informational asymmetry costs, and so offers a potentially plausible explanation for the use of project financing for some projects in fields such as mineral exploration and R&D. The Shah/Thakor premise, however, does not explain the use of project financing for projects that entail low risk and do not require the sponsor to hold back proprietary information of importance in the correct evaluation of the project. This justification for the use of project financing, therefore, cannot be considered universal.

Project Financing Enhances Financial Flexibility. Now let us turn to a more subtle result of project financing: the enhancement of financial flexibility in funding new growth opportunities within the sponsoring firm. We propose that the informational asymmetry approach can be an even more fruitful avenue for attacking the problem of understanding the attraction of project financing if attention is shifted away from the project being funded and refocused onto the other projects in the opportunity set of the corporate sponsor.

Suppose that at the same time a company has a transparent project opportunity, it also has the potential to generate other opportunities about which management has important information that cannot be made available to investors. Then, as Myers and Majluf point out, it would be advisable for the firm to reserve its cash flow from established operations in order to fund these opportunities. All forms of external financing are subject to informational asymmetry costs, but some are less so than others—which has led to the "pecking order" hypothesis that internal cash flows are preferable for financing secret projects,[30] followed in descending order of preference by secured debt and unsecured debt, with equity being least desirable.[31]

The corporation's internal cash flows and unused secured borrowing power thus represent an option that can be used to take advantage of opportunities that would otherwise impose unrecoverable informational asymmetry costs. This option can be preserved by taking advantage of opportunities to sell transparent projects when a fair price can be obtained (that is, few if any informational asymmetry costs are incurred). Choosing project financing in situations that entail low informational asymmetry costs preserves the company's internal financing capacity for use in future projects that have the potential to generate high informational asymmetry costs, thus enhancing the value of the company's growth options.[32]

The value of financial flexibility depends directly upon the prospects for the company to possess valuable growth opportunities in the near future, which will require management to hold back information. Thus the firms with the best prospects will be the ones that find project financing most attractive for their transparent projects. Management's decision to use project financing, therefore, can be interpreted as a positive signal about its evaluation of the firm's growth prospects in other areas.

RECENT USE OF PROJECT FINANCING ARRANGEMENTS

We have built a data base containing information concerning $43.9 billion worth of project financing arrangements in the

United States (representing 585 individual projects). This data includes all of the project financings announced in the *Wall Street Journal* from January 1, 1981 to September 30, 1990, as well as information collected by the U.S. Commerce Department concerning project financing for research and development. We have also collected information from company press releases, project finance specialists, and major electric power project developers. Although our data base is the most comprehensive available on the subject, many privately placed project financings are not announced, so there are undoubtedly some projects yet to be added.[33]

Types of Activities That Utilize Project Financing

Exhibit 8 shows the distribution of projects by size, Exhibit 9 gives information about the types of activities represented by these project financings. All of these projects fall within the low end of the risk spectrum, so the use of project financing cannot be explained by the risk-sharing hypothesis.

The largest single category of projects is composed of electric power cogeneration facilities installed on the site of an industrial plant that uses a substantial amount of steam in its day-to-day operations (oil and gas production, refining, gas transmission, chemicals, food processing, and textiles).[34] The majority of these projects are not large (many are smaller than $25 million, with very few exceeding $200 million). Project sizes range from less than $1 million to $4.1 billion, and the median project size is $32.0 million. Multibillion-dollar projects are the exception rather than the rule. Large project size, therefore, is not the reason project financings have been utilized by companies such as du Pont, ARCO, Texaco, Sun Oil, and Union Carbide. Although the major corporations in the petrochemical complex regularly make investments in new plant and equipment on this scale, the list of companies that have chosen project financing for their cogeneration facilities includes du Pont, ARCO, Texaco, Sun Oil, and Union Carbide.

Exhibit 8
Distribution of Projects by Size

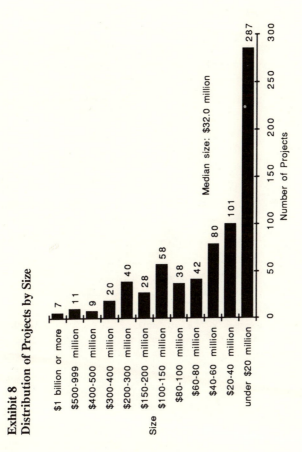

Exhibit 9
Project Financings Announced January 1, 1981 through September 30, 1990

Power Production Project Financings

Cogeneration	$18,752.3 million	16,683.2 megawatts	144 projects
Hydroelectric	$ 3,272.5 million	1,051.8 megawatts	36 projects
Geothermal	$ 1,715.8 million	737.8 megawatts	18 projects
Solar	$ 1,066.6 million	353.8 megawatts	9 projects
Wood-fired	$ 748.0 million	368.6 megawatts	18 projects
Waste-fired	$ 514.5 million	188.8 megawatts	7 projects
Wind	$ 253.2 million	139.8 megawatts	5 projects
Sub-Total	$26,322.8 million	19,523.7 megawatts	237 projects
Average Size	$ 111.1 million	82.4 megawatts	
Largest Project	$ 2,323.5 million	1,370.0 megawatts	
Smallest Project	$ 0.5 million	0.07 megawatts	

Other Project Financings

Oil & Gas Development	$11,524.7 million	67 projects
Real Estate Development	$ 8,204.9 million	75 projects
Plant Construction	$ 6,771.5 million	41 projects
R&D Partnerships	$ 3,705.7 million	239 projects
Mining	$ 3,008.0 million	16 projects
Miscellaneous	$ 7,859.1 million	40 projects
Sub-Total	$41,073.8 million	484 projects
Average Size	$ 84.9 million	
Largest Project	$ 4,100.0 million	
Smallest Project	$ 1.0 million	
Grand Total	$67,396.6 million	721 projects

Furthermore, these projects are clearly at the very low end of the risk spectrum. Due to regulatory requirements, the sponsors of cogeneration projects typically enter into long-term, fixed-price contracts to sell the electricity to a utility for distribution (these contracts generally have a time horizon of 20 years or more). Fuel is sometimes derived from waste products of the host plant; and if not, sources are obtained under long-term, fixed-price contracts. The operation of these plants (which require only about half-a-dozen personnel to operate and maintain) is typically arranged under long-term, fixed-price contracts. Furthermore, it is common practice for engineering firms to offer construction on a fixed-price, turnkey basis, with performance bonding to insure completion according to specifications. As long as the contractual obligations are met, the project's cash flows are stable and predictable. Thus, a potential investor's primary concern is the credit-worthiness of the various parties to the contracts.

Moreover, these project entities can be characterized as clearinghouses for packages of commodity forward contracts. Such packages of contracts can readily be securitized in the form of a project financing. When viewed in this light, project financing is not an isolated phenomenon, but part of the much larger trend of asset securitization.[35]

Nor does the Shah/Thakor informational asymmetry argument explain the use of project financing for cogeneration projects. Detailed information about each one is readily available to the public. Cogeneration technologies are well established and the equipment is highly reliable. Costs for construction, operation, and maintenance are eminently predictable and several institutional investors have developed in-house expertise in project evaluation. Licenses must be obtained from the Federal Energy Regulatory Commission, which gathers details about site-specific technical factors. Finally, federal law requires long-term contracts for the sale of electricity, which are executed in standard forms and are matters of public record.

All that has been said about the size, risk, and information availability for cogeneration projects also holds for the renewable fuels facilities. Moreover, these two categories account for more than half of the total dollars involved in project financings.

The next largest category after electric power production is real estate development. In this category we have included only those limited-recourse project financings that were announced via tombstone advertisements in the *Wall Street Journal* and that involved new developments (as opposed to the acquisition of existing properties). None of the publicly traded real estate partnerships, or REITs, have been included. The data base includes 58 real estate projects, and the mean average size is $121 million. To qualify for limited-recourse financing, lenders require credit support in the form of long-term leases from "anchor tenants" in the case of office developments. In the case of hotel projects, lenders require a prime location (such as a major resort area) in combination with long-term contracts from the hotel operator to lease a substantial block of rooms from the project. Once again, then, the project financing arrangement involves the securitization of long-term contracts, with the primary source of risk for the lenders being the credit-worthiness of the counterparties.

The oil and gas development project financings in our data base also include only those limited-recourse project financings that were announced via tombstone advertisements in the *Wall Street Journal* and that involved new developments (as opposed to the acquisition of existing properties). None of the master limited partnerships or royalty trusts have been included. The data base includes 26 oil and gas projects, with an average size of $146 million. Limited-recourse project loans are typically restricted to development of fields with proven potential.

Limited-recourse project financing also has been used for several manufacturing plants that produce generic products—plants that derive their competitive advantage from the low-risk strategy of applying proven technology (in the form of state-of-the-art automation) to achieve low-cost production of a commodity product. The data base includes 21 plant construction projects, with an average size of $170 million. These were all announced via tombstone advertisements in the *Wall Street Journal.* All of these arrangements involved the highly automated production of generic commodity-type products and included long-term contracts for the purchase of inputs and the sale of output. A German syndicate, for example, financed the construction and operation of a gypsum fiber-board plant being built in Rhode Island, using technology that has already been well established in Europe (this plant is its first American application, under exclusive license). In addition, project financing has been arranged to build and operate paper mills, coil-coating plants (which coat refrigeration coils under contracts with appliance makers), and beverage can production facilities.

Project financing by means of limited partnerships has even been used in research and development, albeit in projects with the emphasis on development as opposed to basic research. Although the thought of R&D often conjures associations with high risk, the kind of projects typically funded in this way do not conform to the high-risk stereotype. In order to structure an R&D partnership that will not only qualify for favorable income tax treatment but also pass the scrutiny of sophisticated investors, it is essential to be able to define property rights for patents that are to be developed for particular products or processes. That is, the base technology must already be in hand, and the steps necessary to develop it—in the jargon of the Internal Revenue Code, "reduce it to a patent"—must be reasonably straightforward. Investing in such a development process, therefore, does not fit the high-risk stereotype. These arrangements are discussed in more detail later in the book.

From these observations we conclude that project financing arrangements typically are not used to shield the sponsor from risk exposure or to reduce the costs of informational asymmetry arising from the project itself. Although these hypotheses are logically consistent with the occasional large-scale venture, they do not explain the many small-scale, low-risk projects that dominate the field of project financing.

Trends in Project Financing

Far from being a recent innovation, project financing is arising from a period of dormancy. Venture-by-venture financing was the norm in commerce until the nineteenth century (and we have found historical references to a limited-recourse lease arrangement for an English silver mining venture in the year 1299, which is very similar to some modern forms of project financing).[36] Although project financing continued to be used by European consortia after the industrial revolution, the antitrust sentiment in the United States created significant barriers to formal expressions of communities of interest among independent companies.

Besides the recent changes in the enforcement of antitrust laws and the regulation of banks (allowing more freedom in establishing limited-recourse lending arrangements), there have been two specific legal developments that contributed significantly to the return of project financing in the United States. One was the 1974 Supreme Court decision in the case of *Snow v. Commissioner*, which allowed the deduction of research and development expenditures by special-purpose project entities, such as research and development limited partnerships. The U.S. Commerce Department reports that such partnerships were uncommon in the 1970s, but activity increased appreciably by the early 1980s with involvement by a number of corporations (for example, Cummins Engine, Cetus, Paco Pharmaceuticals, Nova Pharmaceuticals, Genentech, Beckton-Dickinson, and Emerson Electric). In 1984 several investment banking firms became active in the pooling of R&D projects under the management of in-house R&D management groups.[37]

An even greater impetus for the renewal of project financing came with the Public Utility Regulatory Policy Act (PURPA) of 1978, which requires utilities to purchase electricity from independent, federally licensed generating facilities. Specifically designed to encourage the formation of joint ventures and partnerships for cogeneration and renewable fuels facilities, the law was subjected to numerous challenges by special-interest groups until it was finally upheld by the U.S. Supreme Court in 1982. From that point, project financing for electric power generation projects grew rapidly. With this catalyst, furthermore, specialized project financing groups developed within several investment banking firms, commercial banks, and institutional investors. Then in August 1988 General Electric Capital Corporation announced the formation of a new industrial project financing group. Since its formation it has become GE's fastest-growing unit, and has arranged project financing to build the nation's largest beverage can production plant, as well as several newsprint plants.

Project Financing Dominates the Field of Independent Electric Power Production

In the other areas in which we have observed the use of project financing, it still plays a minor role compared with traditional internal financing arrangements. In the case of independent power production projects, however, project financing has quickly come to dominate the whole field. This arena therefore offers fruitful opportunities for testing hypotheses about the use of project financing.

These projects represent a unique set of "cookie cutter" projects that closely resemble each other. They use established technologies, are highly automated, and require a minimal staff to operate. Moreover, operating costs are generally stabilized via five-year or longer fixed-price operating contracts. Their output of electricity and steam can clearly be categorized as commodities, which uniformly are sold under long-term (20 years or more is common), fixed-price contracts issued by the local utility that buys the electricity and the site owner, which buys the steam for use in its production processes.

A project financing for one of them is essentially a bundle of forward contracts for commodities such as natural gas, coal, thermal and electric energy. The project entity is the counterparty for all the contracts entered into by the various participants, and so performs the function of clearinghouse. Project financing arrangements are preferred when the costs of contracting and enforcing arm's-length agreements among independent entities are less than the costs of conventional financing within a fully integrated corporation.

Thus these projects provide a classic example of the kind of activity Williamson describes as being governed by rules as opposed to management discretion. If financial contracts that impose relatively rigid rules are optimal for financing projects governed by rules, one would expect rule-based financing arrangements to predominate. The null hypothesis is that the type of financial contracting observed for these projects is random.

We therefore obtained data from the Federal Energy Regulatory Commission (FERC) concerning all independent (that is, non-utility) electric power production facilities licensed through the end of 1987.[38] Total generating capacity licensed to non-utility producers is given in Exhibit 10.

Among hydropower, geothermal, and solar facilities, nearly all installations are licensed to independent, project-specific entities. The single solar facility licensed to a corporate entity, moreover, is a small research facility owned by ARCO. (In the case of wind power, there are no exceptions to independent ownership, so this category is omitted from Exhibit 10.) Of the 1,705 cogeneration installations, only 206 are in the name of a *Fortune* 500 corporation. Only 169 more installations with over 1,000 kilowatts of capacity are in the name of a smaller industrial corporation. The remaining 75 percent of total cogeneration capacity is licensed to independent, project-specific entities or individual developers. The preference for project financing is even more pronounced at the large end of the capacity scale. Of the cogeneration facilities over 80 megawatts in size, 124 are organized independently, while only 20 are licensed in the name of a *Fortune* 500 company, and only 6 are licensed to an industrial company smaller than *Fortune* 500 status.

Exhibit 10
Generating Capacity of Non-Utility Electric Power Production Facilities Licensed Through 1987

	Generating Capacity (in megawatts)			
	Cogeneration	Hydro	Geothermal	Solar
Fortune 500 Companies	7,103.6 (16.9%)	93.0 (3.1%)	9.0 (0.4%)	1.4 (0.4%)
Smaller Industrial Corporations	3,068.3 (7.3%)	32.2 (1.1%)	14.0 (0.7%)	0.0 (0.0%)
Independent Projects	31,775.4 (75.8%)	2,873.8 (95.8%)	2,122.2 (98.9%)	377.3 (99.6%)
All FERC filings 1980-1987	41,947.3 (100%)	2,999.0 (100%)	2,145.2 (100%)	378.7 (100%)

Source: Federal Energy Regulatory Commission.

The bonding of cash flows inherent in such arrangements should, according to Jensen, enhance the value of "cash cow" projects that involve high front-end costs (but relatively low operating costs), hold the prospect of depletion of value as they run their course, and spawn few growth opportunities that require the original project as a foundation.[39] Williamson offers a complementary argument, leading to the conclusion that project financing should be value-enhancing for ventures that lend themselves to governance by rules and contracts, as opposed to the discretion of management. An extraordinarily stable and comprehensive contracting environment exists in the independent electric power production activities, so the dominance of project financing in this area accords with Williamson's theoretical analysis.

COMMUNITIES OF INTEREST IN PROJECT FINANCING

In a variety of situations, project financing arrangements have offered a low-cost alternative to merging as a means for creating a structure within which costs and benefits generated for several parties can be internalized within a "community of interests." Without some such structure, in many cases, there would have been so many externalities that no single party would have found the project attractive.

Mutual Benefits in Cogeneration

Commercial cogeneration of electricity represents a joint venture in that it requires the capability, not only to sell electricity, but to use the left-over heat for some commercial purpose, such as process steam for a chemical plant or oil refinery, enhanced oil recovery, or for heating a military installation or a college campus. A utility acting on its own cannot use the steam, however, because the scope of its activities is limited by regulators. Likewise, an industrial corporation acting on its own cannot sell electricity to consumers; nor are the two free to merge. In fact, Congress enacted PURPA in 1978 because few (if any) individual economic entities then in existence were capable of internalizing the benefits of cogeneration, along with the costs. PURPA was aimed at making it possible for the ones who incurred the cost of cogeneration to be able to realize its benefits, so that it could attract private capital.[40]

The decision to invest in cogeneration represents a diversification of the firm's product line in order to exploit potential synergies with existing activities. Cogeneration can enhance the productivity of a variety of installations (including chemical plants, paper mills, oil fields, food processing plants, textile mills, and lumber mills), possibly making the difference between closing a plant and keeping it open. Union Carbide, for example, touting the cogeneration facility at its Seadrift plant in Texas, said, "The improved economics provided by reduced energy costs improves the job security of all of our plant employees."[41] The utility company in turn benefits from higher employment and commercial activity in its region. It also benefits from greater planning flexibility due to shorter construction lead times for cogeneration plants.[42]

As a separate entity, moreover, the project's credit is even better than that of the companies with which it contracts. As argued earlier, if the utility were to go bankrupt, the project would enjoy the status of a supplier, rather than of a creditor; and would continue to sell its electricity to the reorganized utility. If the host plant were to shut down and default on its obligations, on the other hand, project financing would again prove advantageous. The major expense for a normal cogeneration facility involves a few large pieces of machinery, which can easily be shipped to a new site.[43] An independent cogeneration project has few employees who depend solely upon it for their livelihood (sometimes none) and few claims by other stakeholders. Thus, the courts can deal with the liquidation of an independent project much more expeditiously than would be the case if it were part of a corporate package. Project financing therefore enhances the inherent flexibility of the equipment, making it cheaper and quicker to exercise the redeployment option.

To some people in the utility business cogeneration is a four-letter word, because it transforms major customers into suppliers blessed with the protection of federal regulators. Such transformations have, for example, coincided with efforts on the part of the rate-setting agency to force industrial customers to subsidize low rates for households. In other cases, the transformation has been made in the wake of frustrated efforts to get the utility to guarantee a minimum service level.[44] There need not be an adversarial relationship between the cogeneration plant's host and the local utility, however. Instead, project financing for cogeneration facilities can enable the utility company to share in the profit. For example, when Sun Energy and Exploration Company made plans in 1987 to build a 225-megawatt cogeneration project in conjunction with the steam generation plant at its Midway-Sunset Field in California (where the steam is used for enhanced oil recovery), it formed a 50-50 partnership with Mission Energy, an unregulated subsidiary of Southern California Edison.[45]

The use of project financing can also reduce regulatory problems for utilities. If a generation facility were financed by a regulated utility within the corporate umbrella, it would be necessary to demonstrate the cost of equity capital to the regulators when the plant comes on line. In a project financing, the facility is constructed by a separate entity, which sells electricity under a contract approved by the regulators prior to construction. The problem of setting adequate rates is therefore diminished.[46]

Although these jumbo facilities represent large capital investments, they are not particularly risky; nor are the major corporations in the petrochemical complex averse to making investments in new plant and equipment on this scale. The dominance of project financing for the larger sites reflects their extensive joint venture nature more than it does their size. Along the Houston Ship Channel, for example, there are many refineries and petrochemical plants in close proximity to one another; and the area contains ten independently owned cogeneration facilities with capacity in excess of 200 megawatts each. Such large-scale cogeneration facilities can supply steam to several neighboring plants, while offering greater efficiency than would be possible if each plant had its own installation.[47]

Mutual Benefits in Manufacturing

General Electric Capital Corporation recently announced the expansion of its project finance group to specialize in financing the construction and operation of industrial facilities. Earlier in 1988, GE Capital did something that provides a glimpse of the kind of projects it will be underwriting, when it provided limited-recourse project financing ($105 million in all) to build the BevPak beverage container plant. BevPak was founded in January

1988 by a former USX executive. The Monticello, Indiana, plant makes beverage cans, but is independent of any beverage producer. BevPak now has three state-of-the-art production lines running, each with a capacity of 1,600 steel beverage cans per minute. Adjusted for downturn, BevPak's capacity is 2 billion cans a year, or about 40 percent of the total steel beverage can output in the United States. It has contracts with Coca-Cola and Pepsi for as much as 20 percent of their canning needs. It also has a contract with Miller Brewing Company, and Anheuser-Busch is studying a switch to steel cans. BevPak's competitive edge comes, not only from the economies of automation, but from its ability to take advantage of the lower cost of tin-plated steel cans compared to aluminum, while possessing the flexibility to switch to aluminum if the price drops.[48]

Much of the risk associated with financing such a large and highly automated plant arises from uncertainty about whether it will be able to operate at full capacity, and independent ownership enables it to enter arms-length agreements to supply competing beverage makers, giving it the flexibility to operate at a profitable level of output without depending on any single brand's success.[49] For a proprietary bottler, moreover, entering into long-term agreements for a portion of the output from such a plant is a cost-effective alternative to building a smaller one in-house.

GE Capital has also been involved in project financings for newsprint plants, which derive the substance of their credit support from long-term contracts with several major newspapers. One that was announced in October 1989, for example, was essentially a joint venture led by the *New York Times* and the *Washington Post*.

Another recent industrial project financing is the joint venture between Chrysler and Mitsubishi (dubbed "Diamond-Star Motors") to build a new automobile plant in Illinois, which raised $500 million of the $700 million total cost through nonrecourse loans from Japanese banks. With more than 470 robots, this futuristic plant possesses ten times the level of assembly automation found in most auto plants.[50] The chances of profitable

operation for this innovative facility are enhanced by its access to
the know-how and marketing organizations of two auto companies.

Mutual Benefits in Mineral Exploration

Nonrecourse lending arrangements have long been used to
finance large natural resource projects involving several parties;
and no discussion of project financing would be complete
without mention of the Trans-Alaska Pipeline project, a joint
venture among Standard Oil Company (Ohio), Atlantic Rich-
field, Exxon, British Petroleum, Mobil Oil, Phillips Petroleum,
Union Oil, and Amerada Hess Company. The pipeline was
financed through separately incorporated subsidiaries, SOHIO
Pipeline Corporation and BP Pipelines, Inc. SOHIO raised over
$970 million, most of its share in the cost of the pipeline and
tanker fleet, through revenue bonds (issued through the Valdez
Marine Terminal Authority), reserved production agreements,
and tanker leases.[51]

A more recent joint venture was announced in mid-July to
develop a major oil field off the coast of Newfoundland. Hibernia
Oil Field Partners is a joint venture partnership, with Mobil Oil
of Canada slated to serve as managing general partner and project
operator. Other partners include Gulf Canada Resources, Inc.,
Petro-Canada, and the Canadian units of Chevron Oil and
Columbia Gas. The field, which will cost $4.1 billion (U.S.) to
develop, is expected to produce 110,000 barrels of oil a day
starting in 1995. Located 195 miles southeast of St. John's,
Newfoundland, it holds an estimated 525 to 650 million barrels,
giving it an expected productive life of from 16 to 20 years.[52]

Some might consider such a big oil venture to be a dicey
investment in today's climate, but the project offers other benefits
that will flow long before the first drop of oil. It offers jobs and
economic stimulus to a stubbornly depressed region, and so will
generate secondary benefits years before the first royalty check.
Furthermore, it will open the door for development of other nearby

fields, creating options that can be exercised if the price of oil takes an unexpected upward turn. Because of the widespread benefits beyond the scope of the partners, both the Canadian federal government and the Newfoundland provincial government are taking a substantial role, seeing this as a potentially productive alternative to paying unemployment compensation.

The Canadian federal government will provide 2.7 billion Canadian dollars (US$2.23 billion) in grants and loan guarantees. This breaks down to a commitment to pay 25 percent of the construction costs, up to a maximum of $1.04 billion (Canadian), and as much as C$1.66 billion in nonrecourse loans. In return, it will get 10 percent of the project's profits after all loans and interest assistance have been repaid. The Newfoundland provincial government will forego most sales tax for the project's purchases and take a cut in royalties from production.[53]

Why was it done this way, and not with more conventional methods of corporate finance? First of all, the project is too big and risky for any of the partners to tackle alone. More critical, though, is the problem that none of the individual players, acting alone, could capture enough benefits to make the project worthwhile. Columbia Gas, for example, has been seeking a buyer for its Canadian transmission unit, which will transport the natural gas from the Hibernia field. With the project under way, its long-term prospects are brighter, making it a more attractive buy. No doubt, Columbia would have been delighted to see the project go ahead with someone else's money, if that were forthcoming.

Many individuals, small companies, and communities will prosper as a result of the project, and they too would have been delighted to get a free ride. It took government agencies, however, to translate the prospective increases in future tax revenues into funding to offset the cost of the project.

Mutual Benefits in R&D

NaTec, Ltd., a 50-50 partnership between CRS Sirrine and Industrial Resources, Inc. was recently formed to develop a process that will use nahcolyte (a mineable, naturally occurring form of sodium bicarbonate) to clean up the emissions from coal-fired power plants.[54] The process promises to be cheaper and more efficient than current techniques. CRS Sirrine is a respected, NYSE-listed construction and engineering company that builds and upgrades power plants, so the potential benefits to it are obvious. Industrial Resources (IR) is an over-the-counter company with practically no sales or operations—but it owns leases to large deposits of nahcolyte.

If Sirrine had gone ahead with the project alone, IR would have gotten a valuable free ride; but in order to make the project attractive, IR had to share in the costs as well as the benefits. One solution would have been to merge the two companies; but even if that were possible, it would have created complications beyond the scope of the nahcolyte project. A simple joint venture, however, was enough to create an entity that could internalize enough benefits from the project to justify the cost.

NETWORK ORGANIZATIONS

Companies are also learning to work together through temporary, project-specific liaisons, or dynamic networks,[55] which may use project financing for R&D. Dynamic networks thrive in fast-changing environments, such as consumer electronics and apparel. One of them, the sports shoe marketer, Nike, has become quite well known. Nike contracts its manufacturing to offshore factories, itself serving as developer and marketer of products.[56]

As product life cycles compress in response to continuing advances in computer-assisted design (CAD) and computer-integrated manufacturing (CIM), more of the business world is being transformed into the natural habitat of the dynamic networks. Even in auto manufacturing, the bastion of traditional industrial organization, product life cycles are compressing. It used to take five years or more to bring a new automobile to market. Ford Motor Company has cut that to two years. It will keep getting shorter.

In networks of the future, the work might be done by professional firms (much like law firms or accounting firms) specializing in research, product design, or marketing. Manufacturing would be contracted out to offshore factories or to flexible automated factories near the final market. Finally, the key role of putting all the pieces together would go to specialized brokers, perhaps a new breed of investment bankers.

Recent experiments with partnership forms of organization may be laying the foundations of a new way of financing dynamic networks. Only time, of course, will tell the extent to which it will displace integrated corporations. In this alternative, investors still enjoy limited liability but relinquish much less power to managers. Investors are the direct recipients of cash flows from mature operations. They are then free to choose whether or not they wish to provide funding for the development of new products by participating directly in R&D project financing. If development efforts are successful, the rights may be sold or licensed to a manufacturer/marketer. Alternatively, investors may choose to participate in manufacturing and marketing by means of other partnerships.

Recently, with strong encouragement and support from the U.S. Department of Commerce, a few firms have experimented with limited partnerships formed for the purpose of promoting and marketing a specific product. Energy Sciences Corporation offers an example. It recently developed a data networking system that sends data via low-frequency radio signals over existing phone or power lines, while leaving normal utility services undisturbed. The development was funded through project financing. Now the company is preparing a marketing campaign financed by what it calls "technology marketing partnerships."[57]

These marketing partnerships are in essence very simple. They are business organizations formed for the purpose of bringing a specific product or group of products to market. The general partner may manufacture the product or contract it to a third party. The general partner also contracts with third parties for advertising and promotion. The partnership owns the trademark and brandname supported by its advertising, and has an exclusive distributorship for the product. It earns revenues from royalties or commissions paid out of sales by the manufacturer. In some cases they are set up with an option for the manufacturer to buy out the distributorship for a lump sum.

There can be tax advantages generated by these arrangements, but they also provide a project-specific organizational alternative to the corporation. It is possible for a product to be developed by a partnership and brought to market by another partnership, with heavy reliance upon capital raised in the public market. In such a complex of small, specialized organizations the primary role of managers would be to run existing operations efficiently. In order to increase the assets under their management, they would have to compete by creating alluring new opportunities to be offered in the marketplace for capital.

PROJECT FINANCING FOR R&D PROVIDES A LOWER-COST ALTERNATIVE TO MERGER

All is not lost, however, for big established companies. Whenever they have strong competitive advantages from economies of scale in production or marketing, they have much to gain by cooperating with startups or design consultants that have new technologies to offer. It seems that large corporations have the opportunity to benefit from letting small, nimble, low-cost organizations develop new products and technologies, so long as they themselves have strengths to offer in manufacturing or marketing. No less than the giant IBM, moreover, has recently undertaken a massive shift in focus, redeploying its resources from design and manufacturing to marketing and customer service.[58] When the large organizations have an edge in manufacturing or marketing, they may continue to prosper despite declining in-house R&D. The integrating core, however, will no longer be a common technological base, but instead will be a common manufacturing, distribution, or marketing base. Yet the long term may bring continuing pressure upon large corporations because these advantages, too, will melt away for some companies as automated manufacturing spreads and as mass markets fragment.

The advent of practical computer-integrated manufacturing systems in widespread use, on the horizon perhaps as early as the mid-90s, will erode the advantages of large size in many areas of manufacturing, since such systems erase economies of scale and in their place bring tremendous economies of scope.[59] Even one of today's somewhat primitive CIM cells can produce any one of several hundred different parts, at the same cost per unit whether the production run is for a hundred units or only one unit.[60] As such CIM cells become widespread and the bugs are smoothed out, the cost advantage will no longer be with large centrally located factories, but instead will be with networks of small geographically dispersed flexible factories that are close to final markets.[61]

Besides flexibility and low cost, furthermore, the new systems offer superior quality. Because of this, Robert Kaplan recently warned that companies that choose not to invest in the new manufacturing technologies may find themselves in the unenviable position of being high-cost producers of inferior products. These flexible factories, moreover, will be capable of producing a broad range of goods under license to different designers.

Thus, the familiar specialized factories of today (such as "car factories" or "radio factories") will give way to generalized factories that are the new-age analogue of the village blacksmith— they will produce many of our basic goods locally, and the local factory may well not be owned by any particular product designer. Such factories will really be more like utilities. With quality (that is, conformity to design specifications) assured within tight tolerances, competition will be on the basis of product design, where the edge seems to belong to organizations that are small enough to be flexible and provide an environment that is conducive to creativity.

The advantages of mass marketing may also be eroding, with the fragmentation of the media. Cable and satellite television, VCR technology, and specialization within the print media have reduced the value of a blanket advertising appeal to the mass market and enhanced the value of focusing on a particular audience. Campbell's Soup, a pioneer in mass marketing during the early days of radio, for example, has recently begun shifting to a regional and ethnic focus in its product line.

SUMMARY

Project financing can have important restructuring effects. First of all, a project financing represents a community of interests which offers a cost-effective alternative to merger when two or more firms wish to join forces in pursuit of a specific project opportunity. In this regard it is not only useful to large, publicly held corporations but to networks of small, closely held firms, which are becoming increasingly potent competitors against the traditional integrated corporations. In addition, project financing provides a means for direct investment in depleting properties while establishing clear contractual obligations for the return of capital over the life of the project. Current technological trends suggest a growing domain for project financing in the near future.

Empirical observation reveals that the existing theory of project financing does not explain the majority of occurrences, which involve relatively low-risk projects that are transparent in the sense that substantial information about them is readily available to the public. This can be partially resolved by recognizing that project financing arrangements are typically joint ventures that involve a community of interests among several parties. Therefore, no single rationale can adequately explain project financing, since each party must gain something from the arrangement. We have examined several sources of benefit for the various participants, including substantial benefits to the investors in the form of tax savings and reduced agency costs of free cash flow.

In addition, we hypothesize that firms with attractive growth prospects in areas that must be kept secret from competitors will find project financing particularly attractive for their more commonplace activities, such as electric power cogeneration. Thus the choice of project financing for commonplace activities sends a positive signal that the corporation possesses valuable growth opportunities. This hypothesis is supported by the evidence that project financing dominates the field of independent electric power generation, where the technology and regulatory environment are such that most of the information about the project is publicly available.[62]

In closing, we wish to emphasize that project financing involves the choice of an alternative organizational form, which differs substantially from the traditional indefinite-lived corporation and should not be treated simply in terms of leverage—it is more than a variation on the capital structure question. Project financing cannot be plotted on a continuum reflecting different proportions of project financing for a given venture—the project is either financed as an independent entity, or it is not. Furthermore, project financing utilizes finite-lived organizational forms whose identities are firmly linked to specific facilities. Cash flows from the project, including depreciation and depletion, are paid out directly to investors, who make the reinvestment decisions themselves.

Thus project financing has the potential to fundamentally alter the role of management. The lure of enhanced financial flexibility, as well as reduced regulatory and legal costs, attracts corporate management to establish new cash cow projects as independent entities. Subsequently, however, the cash flows from these projects are committed to be disgorged; and thus as the corporation matures, the free cash flows available within it are diminished. This leads to managers becoming increasingly associated with the operation of specific projects or the development of new ones to be offered to the market, while the reinvestment decisions—and the final say in long-term strategic planning that go with them—are returned to the investment community. In the wake of this transition, entrepreneurs with plans that must be kept secret from competitors will need to form value-adding partnerships with discrete financiers.

NOTES

1. When the revenues to be derived from a new municipal project offer more stability than the general revenues of a municipality, the cost of capital can be reduced by isolating the project from the general pool. Given the political hurdles to overcome in making a project happen, the ability to point to a low cost of capital can be a selling point (even if, theoretically, the low-risk project would reduce the municipality's overall cost of capital).

2. See John Kensinger and John Martin, "Project Financing," pp. 69–81, for a summary of the early history of project financing and the reasons for its period of quiescence.

3. From January 1, 1981 through February 28, 1990, underwriters have announced over $43.9 billion worth of project financings—an amount of financing equivalent to the formation of a new company in the upper echelon of the *Fortune* 500. The average of $835 million in announced project financings per month during 1988 and 1989 compares with an average of $30.2 billion per month of new securities (both debt and equity) issued by all U.S. corporations (sources: IDD Information Services, Inc., U.S. Securities and Exchange Commission, and the Board of Governors of the Federal Reserve System). Given that many project financings are not advertised by their underwriters, it is evident that project financing deserves to be taken seriously.

4. Project financing has become widespread among companies in oil and gas production, refining, gas transmission, chemicals, food processing, and textiles.

5. Many project financings are relatively small. There have been several all-equity R&D partnerships in the $20 to $50 million range, and there have been numerous leveraged hydroelectric project financings in the same size range. Whereas the hydroelectric projects generate stable, predictable cash flows that can support a relatively heavy load of fixed-debt-support obligations, the R&D projects tend to be less predictable, and so utilize a different structure of obligations.

6. Later in the chapter we offer evidence showing that project financing has quickly become the dominant form of financing for the nearly 2,000 independent electric power generation facilities that have been licensed during the 1980s (both before and after tax reform).

7. For example, Catalyst Energy made effective use of the limited partnership organizational form to structure its electric power generation project financings. The majority of the cost was raised through nonrecourse debt, with most of the remainder provided by limited partnership equity. During the beginning years of a project, the cash flow left after debt support payments was committed to the limited partners. Only after retirement of the debt and return of the limited partner's capital (plus a prearranged minimum

return on investment) would Catalyst Energy, as general partner, begin receiving a significant share of the cash flows. (Thus the limited partners' interest is similar to convertible subordinated debt, while the general partner possesses the residual equity position.) Catalyst chose projects well, and six years after its birth had established a level of cash flow that made it the object of a friendly acquisition, which promises to leave the founders very wealthy.

8. Innovators will undoubtedly find more ways to frame nonrecourse project financings. The key is to establish the project within a finite-lived organizational structure that separates it from its owners yet preserves their control over the reinvestment of capital as it returns from the project.

9. The British Petroleum example is reported in Richard Brealey and Stewart Myers, *Principles of Corporate Finance.*

10. If the development were successful, BP Development would be obligated to deliver the oil on a specified schedule. Thus, this was in essence a reserved production agreement.

11. If British Petroleum produced more oil from the field in any given year than it was required to deliver to Norex, the funds from the sale of the extra oil would be placed in a special account upon which Norex could draw later if future oil deliveries were insufficient to meet debt service obligations.

12. Source: P-H Federal Taxes 1986, Sec. 174, Para. 16,209(17).

13. Source: U.S. Congress, *Congressional Record*, pp. H7633-7.

14. This includes $8.4 billion in oil and gas MLPs and $2.4 billion in real estate MLPs (source: *The Stanger Report*, p. 2). For a thorough discussion of the impact of the new tax law on MLPs, see J. Collins and R. Bey, "The Master Limited Partnership."

15. Jean Gimpel, *The Medieval Machine*, p. 73.

16. It is worth noting that the taking of interest was strictly prohibited throughout the Christian world at the time. Since the bankers were at risk in this venture, however, the arrangement fell within the bounds allowed by canon law. Finding ways to cope with regulators, after all, is nothing new for innovative financiers.

17. The governments, however, levied a requirement. In return for their advantages and privileged position, the trading companies were expected to increase the national wealth. They were protected from domestic competition so they could compete more strongly against their foreign rivals.

18. The venerable British East India Company was chartered in 1600 and endured until 1858 (this truly comes into perspective with the realization that it began before the founding of Jamestown and ended on the eve of the American Civil War). The United Dutch East India Company arose through the 1602 consolidation of ten companies of merchant venturers. French, Spanish, and Portuguese companies were also formed at about the same time. A relative latecomer in 1670, the Hudson's Bay Company continues to this day.

19. E. L. J. Coornaert, *The Cambridge Economic History of Europe*, pp. 223–75.

20. Even before small investors gained access to the stock market in seventeenth-century Amsterdam, a speculative market developed in "nominal" shares. This nominal stock market, located in the coffee houses adjacent to the merchants' exchange, allowed individual investors to trade in forward contracts and options on stock despite attempts by the companies to impose "order" on the trading in their stock. Source: Fernand Braudel, *The Wheels of Commerce*, pp. 101–03.

21. In the ongoing "regulatory dialectic" the exact nature of such arrangements changes over time. Currently, project financings may take the form of general partnerships, limited partnerships, special-purpose corporations, or nonrecourse leases.

22. Even those partnerships which are publicly traded are free of double taxation for a wide range of so-called passive activities. Under §7704 of the Internal Revenue Code (enacted in the Revenue Act of 1987), the list of allowable income sources includes the following activities involving natural resources: exploration, development, mining or production, processing, refining, transportation (including gas or oil pipelines), or the marketing of any mineral or natural resource (including fertilizer, timber, and geothermal energy). In addition there are several other income sources that are commonly understood to be passive for individual income tax purposes: interest, dividends, real property rents or capital gains, and gains from commodities trading for a partnership specializing in such trading (including futures, forwards, and options).

23. When the operational environment of the project is likely to change, however, granting management wide discretion can save frequent (and costly) revision of rules and contracts.

24. For example, it is possible for management to receive considerable pressure to reinvest for the purpose of preserving jobs in a given community, although investors have better alternatives outside the company.

25. Cogeneration is the simultaneous production of electricity and thermal energy (usually in the form of steam), both of which are produced for commercial purposes.

26. We thank Roger Cason of E. I. du Pont de Nemours, Inc., for this insight.

27. In a recent example of the clashes that can occur between banks and regulators over this issue, Citicorp Venture Capital was forced to revamp its plans to purchase the Del Monte canned foods business from RJR Nabisco. See the *Wall Street Journal*, September 19, 1989, p. A4.

28. J. Brickley, R. Lease, and C. Smith, in *Principles of Corporate Finance*, argue the benefits of an ownership stake for management.

29. In oil and gas exploration, for example, project financing could reduce the cost of information acquisition for investors. The geophysical data necessary to estimate the value of oil reserves is difficult to obtain and expensive to analyze. If the project were undertaken as part of a corporate whole, investors in all of the company's outstanding securities would need such information. By isolating the project, however, the need for such information is limited to the investors in the project financing, sparing others the cost of acquiring and processing the information. When bidding is concentrated upon a specific area rather than a pool of geographically dispersed holdings so that the costs of being informed are reduced, furthermore, there are more potential bidders who can afford to become informed, thus enhancing the efficiency of valuation.

30. R. Korajczyk, D. Lucas, and R. McDonald, "The Effect of Information Releases," offer some new evidence in this regard.

31. Even in the best of situations, however, informational asymmetry costs may be incurred temporarily, when investors perceive that cash of a known value is being expended on activities of unknown value. Yet with internal financing, the equity value will have a chance to rebound when the information about the new activities is released.

32. This concept was inspired by a conversation between one of the authors and a money-center banker who specializes in project finance. When asked why project financing is used for electric generation projects, the banker replied simply, "There's a market for it!" He considered it to be obvious that a project should be sold if a fair price can be obtained. This attitude makes sense in the context of the "pecking order" hypothesis, which can be amended to say: sell projects that have low informational asymmetry costs, in order to use internal capital for those that have high informational asymmetry costs.

33. Two very large non-U.S. project financings have been left out of the totals reported here. One is the £7.1 billion (approximately $12.2 billion) Eurotunnel project to dig a tunnel beneath the English Channel by early 1993. The other is the C$5.2 billion (approximately US$4.1 billion) Hibernia Oil Field Partners project to develop a large oil field off the coast of Newfoundland.

34. With cogeneration, the site is chosen to be near an activity that can make commercial use of the heat, and the size of the plant is determined in large part by the site's capacity to use the excess heat. Whereas a stand-alone electrical generation plant is able to convert only about 33 percent of its fuel's available energy into usable output, a cogeneration facility is capable of 70 percent efficiency. People who look for cogeneration opportunities, it has been said, are exploring for oil in the cooling towers of America's utilities; because instead of throwing away left-over heat, cogeneration puts it to work (from comments by Thomas R. Casten, *Energy Utilities*, p. 79).

35. Kensinger and Martin, "Project Financing," pp. 69–81, provide a discussion of project financing in the context of asset securitization.

36. See ibid. for a summary of the early history of project financing and the reasons for its period of quiescence.

37. Merrill Lynch and Prudential-Bache remain active in R&D project management. E. F. Hutton and Morgan Stanley have also been involved in the past.

38. Many of these are not included in the financial data base discussed above. FERC data is technical in nature and does not include financial information. When building our financial data base, we included only those for which we could find a second source of documentation concerning the financial arrangements. The FERC data does, however, identify the licensee by name.

39. Examples include mineral exploration ventures as well as ventures in developing hotels, office buildings, or automated factories. These involve high up-front investment, and then deplete or depreciate. Once used up, old wells are closed, old buildings torn down, and obsolete equipment scrapped. Then the expenditure of funds for replacements is a new investment decision that can be left up to the market.

40. Recognizing the bargaining advantage a utility could wield over cogenerators, PURPA requires regulated utilities not only to purchase cogenerated power at the utility's marginal cost but also supply backup power at nondiscriminatory rates. Small power producers (less than 80 megawatts) using renewable energy sources (i.e., hydro, geothermal, or biomass) were also included, as discussed earlier.

41. Union Carbide News Release, January 22, 1987.

42. The lead time is two to three years for a cogeneration plant, compared with five to seven years for a conventional coal-fired plant—or up to ten years for a nuclear plant.

43. Few sites require more than general-purpose industrial buildings for protection from the elements. Exceptions are generally confined to high-density population areas, such as college campuses.

44. In some circles, cogeneration facilities are even derisively referred to as "PURPA machines," with the implication that they exist only because of favorable tax treatment. The 1986 tax reforms, however, wiped out the accelerated depreciation schedule, investment tax credits, and energy credits that were the basis of such criticism. The continued vitality of project financing for independent power production in the post-reform tax environment is testimony to the underlying economic viability of such ventures.

45. Indeed, all utilities could share in the efficiencies of cogeneration, even without direct participation, if they could negotiate contracts to buy electricity at prices below their own cost of generation. Currently, however, federal regulations require them to pay their own full long-term marginal cost

(called "avoided cost"). This requirement, then, is the true bone of contention, and avoided cost issues are under vigorous debate in such industry forums as *The Public Utilities Fortnightly*, as well as in the corridors of power.

46. If sufficient new capacity cannot be attracted at rates desired by the local regulators, they will face a choice between committing to higher rates or accepting the prospect of shortages. Current practice, in contrast, is for the utility to construct a plant and then wait until the plant comes on line to negotiate a change in the rate base. Clearly, the utility faces uncertainty in this arrangement.

47. For a variety of strategic reasons, competing corporations find it preferable to contract for steam with an independent entity rather than depend upon a competitor to supply their needs.

48. *Wall Street Journal*, June 8, 1989, p. B1.

49. It would be, more agreeable to Pepsi, for example, to contract for containers from an independent producer than to depend upon the excess capacity of a plant owned by Coke.

50. Estimate reported in *Business Week*, September 12, 1988, p. 73.

51. See P. Phillips, J. Groth, and R. Richards, "Financing the Alaskan Project," pp. 7–16, for details.

52. For further reference, Hibernia's estimated reserves represent about 2.4 percent of the total proven reserves in the United States.

53. *Wall Street Journal*, July 19, 1988, p. 17.

54. *Wall Street Journal*, July 27, 1988, p. 4.

55. For a detailed description of dynamic network organizations and predictions for their future role, see Raymond E. Miles and Charles C. Snow, "Network Organizations," pp. 62f.

56. See *Business Week*, March 3, 1986.

57. For more details, see *Financial Planning*, October 1985, pp. 181–88.

58. See Dennis Kneale, "Tough Choices," p. 1. See also Geoff Lewis, "Big Changes at Big Blue," pp. 92f.

59. Economies of scope derive from cost reduction as a result of applying assets to the production of a variety of different products. Economies of scale, in contrast, derive from cost reduction as a result of applying assets intensely to the high-volume production of a small range of products. For the earliest development of ideas about economies of scope, see J. Panzar and R. Willig, "Economies of Scale," and "Economies of Scope," respectively.

60. The CIM cell at General Dynamics in Fort Worth, for example, can produce any of over 500 different aircraft parts, with "retooling" accomplished merely by selecting a different computer program. The automated assembly operation at the IBM plant in Austin, Texas, offers another mind-stretching example. There, the PC Convertible production is done entirely by robots. Machines sort the components, assemble them into finished comput-

ers, perform all systems tests, and pack the new computers in their boxes. Human workers don't enter the scene until it is time to load the finished computers onto trucks for shipment. The assembly system could be readily reprogrammed for a variety of new products.

61. Recent research leads to the disquieting conclusion that many of the "bugs" now troubling some of the American pioneers in CIM are the fault of management rather than the systems themselves. It seems that American managers often try to force CIM into working the "old-fashioned way," with large production runs and little variety. Their Japanese competitors, in contrast, play to the strengths of CIM by utilizing the inherent flexibility in short production runs for a variety of products. In time, U.S. management will either learn to use the flexible systems effectively, or fall by the wayside (see R. Jaikumar, "Postindustrial Manufacturing," pp. 69–76).

62. The technologies involved are well known, and the licensing applications and power purchase contracts are a matter of public record.

REFERENCES

Braudel, Fernand. *The Wheels of Commerce*, Vol. II, *Civilization and Capitalism* (New York: Harper & Row, 1982), pp. 101–3.

Brealey, Richard A., and Stewart C. Myers. *Principles of Corporate Finance* (3rd ed.) (New York: McGraw-Hill Book Company, 1988).

Brickley, J., R. Lease, and C. Smith. "Ownership Structure and Voting on Antitakeover Amendments," *Journal of Financial Economics* 20 (January 1988), pp. 267–91.

Business Week, March 3, 1986.

Business Week, September 12, 1988, p. 73.

Casten, Thomas R. "Comments," *Energy Utilities: The Next Ten Years.* Proceedings of a symposium sponsored by the California Public Utilities Commission at Stanford University, March 27–28, 1981, p. 79.

Collins, J., and R. Bey. "The Master Limited Partnership: An Alternative to the Corporation," *Financial Management* 15 (December 1986).

Coornaert, E. L. J. *The Cambridge Economic History of Europe*, Vol. IV, Chapter IV (Cambridge, England: Cambridge University Press, 1967), pp. 223–75.

Cornell, B., and A. Shapiro. "Corporate Stakeholders and Corporate Finance," *Financial Management* (Spring 1987).

Financial Planning (October 1985), pp. 181–88.

Gimpel, Jean. *The Medieval Machine: The Industrial Revolution of the Middle Ages* (New York: Holt Rinehart Winston, 1976), p. 73.

Hu, S. David. *Cogeneration* (Reston, Va.: Reston Publishing Co., 1985).

Jaikumar, Ramachanran. "Postindustrial Manufacturing," *Harvard Business Review*, Vol. 64, No. 6 (November–December 1986) pp. 69–76.

Jensen, Michael. "Agency Costs of Free Cash Flow," *American Economic Review* (May 1986).

Kaplan, R. "Must CIM Be Justified by Faith Alone?" *Harvard Business Review*, Vol. 64, No. 2 (March–April 1986), pp. 87–97.

Kensinger, John, and John Martin. "Project Financing: Raising Money the Old-Fashioned Way," *Journal of Applied Corporate Finance* (Fall 1988), pp. 69–81.

Kneale, Dennis. "Tough Choices—Cutting Output, IBM Tells Some Workers: Move, Retire, or Quit," *Wall Street Journal*, April 8, 1987, p. 1.

Korajczyk, R., D. Lucas, and R. McDonald. "The Effect of Information Releases on the Pricing and Timing of Equity Issues: Theory and Evidence," Working Paper No. 59 (September 1988), Kellogg School of Management, Northwestern University.

Lewis, Geoff. "Big Changes at Big Blue," *Business Week*, February 15, 1988, pp. 92f.

Mao, James. "Project Financing: Funding the Future," *Financial Executive* (April 1982), pp. 23–28.

Martin, John, and John Kensinger. "An Economic Analysis of R&D Limited Partnerships, "*Midland Corporate Finance Journal*, Vol. 3, No. 4 (Winter 1986), pp. 33–45.

Martin, John, and John Kensinger. "R&D Limited Partnership Financing and the New Tax Law," *Midland Corporate Finance Journal* Vol. 4, No. 4 (Winter 1987), pp. 44–54.

Miles, Raymond E., and Charles C. Snow. "Network Organizations: New Concepts for New Forms," *California Management Review* (Spring 1986), pp. 62f.

Myers, Stewart, and Nicholas Majluf. "Corporate Financing and Investment Decisions When Firms Have Information That Investors Do Not Have," *Journal of Financial Economics* 13 (1984), pp. 187–221.

Panzar, J., and R. Willig. "Economies of Scale and Economies of Scope in Multi-Output Production," Bell Laboratories Economic Discussion Paper No. 33 (1975).

Panzar, J., and R. Willig. "Economies of Scope," Bell Laboratories Economic Discussion Paper No. 197 (1981).

Phillips, P., J. Groth, and R. Richards. "Financing the Alaskan Project: The Experience at Sohio," *Financial Management* 8 (Autumn 1979), pp. 7–16.

Sarmet, Marcel. "Recent Trends in International Project Financing," *The Banker* (September 1981), pp. 123–35.

Shah, Salman, and Anjan Thakor. "Optimal Capital Structure and Project Financing," *Journal of Economic Theory* 42 (1987), pp. 209–43.

The Stanger Report, Vol. 8, No. 9, September 1986, p. 2.

U.S. Congress, *Congressional Record*, September 18, 1986, pp. H7633–7.

Wall Street Journal, July 19, 1988, p. 17.

Wall Street Journal, July 27, 1988, p. 4.

Wall Street Journal, June 8, 1989, p. B1.

Wall Street Journal, September 19, 1989, p. A4.

Williamson, Oliver E. "Corporate Finance and Corporate Governance," *Journal of Finance* 43 (1988), pp. 567–91.

Worenklein, J. "Project Financing of Joint Ventures," *Public Utilities Fortnightly* (December 3, 1981), pp. 39–46.

Government Documents

Board of Governors of the Federal Reserve System

Federal Energy Regulatory Commission (FERC)

IDD Information Services, Inc.

Internal Revenue Code

P-H Federal Taxes 1986, Sec. 174, Para.16,209(17)

Public Utility Regulatory Policy Act (PURPA)

Revenue Act of 1987 (§7704 of the Internal Revenue Code)

Snow v. Commissioner (Supreme Court Decision, 1974)

U.S. Commerce Department

U.S. Securities and Exchange Commission

Miscellaneous

All of the project financings announced in the *Wall Street Journal* from January 1, 1981 to March 31, 1990

Conversation with Roger Cason, March 1989

The Public Utilities Fortnightly Forum

Tombstone advertisements in the *Wall Street Journal*

Union Carbide News Release, January 22, 1987

Chapter 7

Dequity Reflects Changing Relationships Between Managers and Investors

The stockholder is therefore left as a matter of law with little more than the loose expectation that a group of men, under a nominal duty to run the enterprise for his benefit and that of others like him, will actually observe this obligation. In almost no particular is he in a position to demand that they do or refrain from doing any given thing. . . . The legal doctrine that the judgment of the directors must prevail as to the best interests of the enterprise, is in fact tantamount to saying that in any given instance the interests of the individual may be sacrificed to the economic exigencies of the enterprise as a whole.
—Adolph Berle and Gardner Means, 1932[1]

When asked recently what the new decade holds in store for investors, Robert Farrell, chief technical analyst for Merrill Lynch, replied, "I . . . get a sense that the sun is setting on the era of stocks and other financial assets, and that the Nineties will see a new game come to the fore. I'm not sure what the new game will be, but an educated guess might be factories and other productive assets as opposed to pieces of paper."[2]

The last five years have witnessed an unprecedented number of corporate disappearances from the list of the *Fortune* 500—there have been 143 in all—as well as significant downsizing by many of the surviving companies. This has been associated with trends toward paying higher dividends, spinning off divisions into independent status, repurchasing shares, arranging leveraged buyouts, farming out new growth to partially owned subsidiaries, and other forms of corporate "hollowing." Increasingly, investors prefer to own airplanes instead of airlines, oil wells instead of integrated oil companies, timberlands instead of forest products companies, and real estate instead of corporate stock. They often do so by means of financial arrangements that utilize dequity financing, such as limited partnerships, limited-recourse debt, or limited-recourse leases. Such uses of dequity are part of a migration of business activities to new organizational forms. Why are investors showing a preference for greater control over assets? In a nutshell, stock in a widely held corporation has evolved into an odd sort of property, which conveys few enforceable rights to its owners.

Most people conceive of property in terms of traditional—one might even say ancient—legal classifications. Tangible property is either "real" property (in the form of land or rights derived from land) or "personal" property (something capable of being consumed or used, yet mobile and so capable of being moved by its owners or taken away from them). Intangible property is a claim on others that is capable of being enforced in the courts, such as a debt contract. In both instances, the courts and their agents stand ready to enforce the owner's rights to exclusive use of the property and to protect it from unlawful taking. Although property typically derives its substance from the protection of the courts through the due process of law, the courts stand ready to defend the incorporated enterprise as a whole even at the expense of the stockholders. This is not necessarily due to any flagrant disregard for stockholders' rights but reflects a duty to another "person"—the corporate entity itself—which stands before the courts as an entity separate and apart from individual stockholders, employees, or any other specific group of associates in the enterprise. The corporation represents an amalgam of all their interests, along with those of the state which chartered it. Separate entity status for corporations is a long-standing legal principle with roots in Roman law, out of which arose the principle of limited liability for stockholders. Furthermore, by seeking limited liability within the corporate form of organization, thereby disclaiming personal responsibility for corporate acts, shareholders explicitly acknowledge a separate identity for the corporation. Thereafter, any shareholder who seeks to disregard the separate existence of his own creature is likely to meet resistance, not only from management, but also from the courts. *The National Carbide Co.* opinion is often cited in determining whether a principal-agency relationship exists between shareholders and management. The telling distinction boils down to this: "if shareholders [claim limited liability and so] disclaim responsibility for the corporation's activities, they are ipso facto rejecting the status of principals."[3] The Delaware Supreme Court, moreover, upheld the principle that a corporation has a separate existence from stockholders in its controversial August 1989 decision concerning the Time-Warner merger.

Unless stockholders can organize themselves in order to make effective use of their votes (a costly and failure-prone endeavor), they must depend upon market forces to protect their property rights. The logic here—that when enough dissatisfied shareholders sell their stock, the price will drop to the point that it becomes attractive for someone to take over control—is meager consolation for the vast numbers of dissatisfied shareholders who sold on the way down, without whose sacrifice the survivors presumably would not have been able to cash in on the takeover premium. At best this process provides only a slow-working kind of justice for the shareholders as an amorphous group, but no protection at all for the individual shareholder.

There is no other form of property that depends for its substance upon the processes of the marketplace instead of the due process of law. Even so, the courts have frequently intervened to protect corporations *against* the forces of the financial marketplace, and the legislatures of New York, Illinois, Pennsylvania, New Jersey, Ohio, Michigan, Connecticut, Massachusetts, Maryland, Indiana, Minnesota, and Kentucky have enacted anti-takeover laws. The Federal Reserve Board, furthermore, has imposed restrictions (in 1986) on borrowing for purposes of taking over control of a corporation. Small wonder then that investors are quietly turning to direct ownership of productive assets.

AN ENTITY SEPARATE AND APART

Stock in a widely held corporation provides only the most modest of recourse to the courts for protection of property rights. (Stockholders' principal entitlements are the right to receive equal dividends as others in the same class and the pre-emptive right to buy enough new shares to maintain their proportional ownership when more shares are issued.) Although bondholders can sue if an interest payment is missed, stockholders cannot sue if a dividend is omitted. More to the point, this means that a few bondholders can force a corporation into receivership if it is no longer capable of paying an adequate, timely return on capital; but stockholders cannot. A highly leveraged corporation will be quickly terminated once it ceases to be economically viable; but there is little to keep a corporation with a conservative capital structure from wasting away to nothing once it becomes obsolete or overburdened by regulations.

In fact, it is precisely the removal of this right to terminate the enterprise that marks the appearance of the modern publicly held corporation in the annals of history. The corporation as a large-scale, quasi-permanent property owner traces its roots to the impoundment of capital in the Dutch East India Company in 1612—prior to that time any stockholder could redeem his shares on demand at par value from the company treasury. This change in the corporate charter was enacted by the state, not by a vote of shareholders. Of course, it represented a significant increase in the power of the managing directors, who were chosen by the governing bodies of the major Dutch cities. This unprecedented action arose from the difficulty of liquidating assets such as fleets at sea and warehouses half a world away—not to mention treaties negotiated with sovereign heads of state—leading to fears that a panic could ruin the company. It was done out of the belief that strengthening the company would benefit the nation as a whole.

Although shares in the company soon began trading on the merchants' exchange, the directors tried long and hard to regulate this activity, and for many years a sale of stock could not be transacted officially without their approval.

Management's continuing allegiance to the corporate entity, rather than to stockholders, is all too clear in Gordon Donaldson's detailed study of twelve large *Fortune* 500 firms. The managers he observed did not try to maximize shareholders' wealth, but instead sought to maximize "corporate wealth," defined as *"the aggregate purchasing power available to management for strategic purposes during any given planning period.* [emphasis in original] . . . this wealth consists of the stocks and flows of cash and cash equivalents (primarily credit) that management can use at its discretion to implement decisions involving the control of goods and services. . . . In practical terms it is cash, credit, and other corporate purchasing power by which management commands goods and services."[4]

This orientation does not necessarily constitute an indictment of crass self-interest on the part of managers, who understandably feel commitments to many other corporate stakeholders besides the investors who contributed capital.[5] Managers are typically far closer to the corporation's employees, for example, than to the investors. Likewise, they feel closer ties to their host community than they do to a faceless and widely dispersed group of public investors. (In fairness it should be noted that host communities often contribute property as well as tax privileges to the corporation, while employees often contribute effort beyond that commanded by their wages, in the hope of gaining job security.) Managers may even be convinced that building a strong, enduring corporate institution is best for the stockholders in the long run, even in the absence of confirmation from the stock market in the short run.

Moreover, this tension between the interests of the individual shareholders and the enterprise as a whole is rooted in long-standing tradition. By keeping their wealth in highly mobile form, financiers since ancient times have been able to remain aloof from ties to any particular city, region, or even nation. (So long as it is mobile, their wealth can stay in constant use for purposes of promoting productive enterprise.) In the hands of a venturer with vision, money becomes a tool for guiding productive resources into higher-valued uses, developing innovative avenues for commerce and industry—but paradoxically, such people are often feared and despised (in 1759 Quesnay wrote disparagingly about the most powerful merchants of his day as "holders of pecuniary fortunes [who] know neither king nor country").[6] Such freedom is a continual threat to those who are rooted in place—who fear a departure of capital would soon leave their home a desert.

DIRECT INVESTMENT AND "DOWNSIZING"

As if these problems were not enough, however, the separate entity status of corporations is the legal principal upon which corporate income taxation is based.[7] It is clearly undesirable for a tax-sheltered pension fund or a tax-exempt endowment fund to own real estate or capital equipment indirectly via stock in a tax-paying corporation—so long as it is possible to own the assets directly through an arrangement such as a trust or limited partnership, which is able to pass income untaxed directly to its owners. Even those partnerships that are publicly traded are free of double taxation for a wide range of so-called passive activities. Under §7704 of the Internal Revenue Code (enacted in the Revenue Act of 1987), the list of allowable income sources includes the following activities involving natural resources: exploration, development, mining or production, processing, refining, transportation (including gas or oil pipelines), or the marketing of any mineral or natural resource (including fertilizer, timber, and geothermal energy). In addition there are several other income sources that are commonly understood to be passive for income tax purposes: interest, dividends, real property rents or capital gains, and gains from commodities trading for a partnership specializing in such trading (including futures, forwards, and options).

Because the choice of organizational form used for securitizing assets is sensitive to the tax environment, the mechanisms change in accordance with it. The 1987 tax act, for example, levied the requirement that publicly traded partnerships be taxed as corporations; and in the absence of favored tax treatment for publicly traded partnerships, other organizational forms rose to favor as repositories for the assets (for example, a trust or nontraded partnership). This continual give and take between innovative financial engineers and the taxing authorities reflects the regulatory dialectic at work—as fast as the authorities close one avenue, innovators find new ways to carry on.

The primary tax-related problem for an institutional investor in arranging asset acquisition, moreover, is to avoid being considered as an active participant in the business activity, which could expose it to taxation as a corporation (it can own airplanes, for example, but it cannot run an airline). If the exceptions noted above should prove inadequate, an alternative is the leveraged lease arrangement in which a financial entrepreneur takes the equity stake and borrows most of the cost of the equipment from the institution, with the cash flows from the lease agreement providing credit support. Then the institutional lender's risk/reward profile is substantially the same as if it owned the asset directly, when the lender's recourse is for practical purposes limited to the cash flows from the lease and the lessee has substantial freedom of cancellation (American Airlines, for example, has entered into several aircraft leases which allow it substantial freedom to cancel). Tax liabilities arising from the cash flowing through the lease are deferred until the pension fund makes payments to its retirees, and double taxation at the corporate entity level is completely avoided. This tax deferral occurs when the lessee deducts lease payments and the entrepreneur deducts interest expense, but the pension fund is exempt from taxation of its interest earnings.

The downsizing trend has been facilitated by the growing practice of securitizing specialized pools of assets. For example, it is now commonplace for financial institutions to sell insured mortgages in the form of securities. Credit card receivables, auto and truck loans are likewise packaged into high-denomination securities for resale. In addition there are hundreds of limited partnerships that own oil and gas wells, hydro, geothermal, and cogeneration power production facilities, oil refineries, and even factories, as well as timberland properties, cable television systems, real estate, mortgages, restaurant services, and mortgage loan servicing. All sorts of income-producing operations that require little more than caretaker management have been organized as partnerships or other independent entities and funded through limited-recourse project financings. Even management-intensive operations, such as R&D projects, have been financed as separate organizational entities.

Besides the tax advantages, there is an important additional effect as well, in the form of increased managerial accountability. The sale of a corporation's real estate holdings to a trust or limited partnership, for example, or the decision to lease rather than buy equipment, such as ships, aircraft, or factories, can be a particularly potent step in the process of returning resource-allocation decisions to the marketplace. When it owned the property, the corporation might weather a bad year or two without having to confess that it was losing money. Without the necessity of writing rent checks, the management could ignore the fact that the company was not earning enough to justify the space it occupied. After the sale of the company's real estate, though, management would have to give an accounting if the company could not pay its rent.

TODAY'S INVESTORS PRIZE THEIR FREEDOM

The pendulum has swung far in the direction of separating stockholders from their property rights, but a recent headline declared in no uncertain terms, "Mad as hell, institutional investors turn activist."[8] Investors have learned that they need not huddle in perpetual submission to the corporate entity; they can protect themselves. Increasingly activist institutional investors are using their clout to influence the choice of key executives, change corporate strategies, and resist the imposition of anti-take-over devices. Even more significant, many are choosing a far less conspicuous avenue—the exit lane from further investments in corporate securities.

In the public debate about leveraged buyouts and hostile takeovers, which have accounted for most of the disappearances from the *Fortune* 500, the emphasis has tended to focus upon the often-lamented "bust-up" liquidations of corporate assets. These assets don't disappear from the face of the earth, however. Instead, they often end up being directly owned by investors—frequently with no change in function. Hostile takeovers, moreover, are just one highly visible aspect of the realignment of power that is being accomplished through direct ownership of specific productive assets. Over 27 percent of the companies that have disappeared from the *Fortune* 500 did so because downsizing left them too small to be included (23 companies) or shifted the focus of their activities so much that they were reclassified from an industrial company to a service company (another 16 companies).

Direct ownership not only reduces risk by providing investors with more-enforceable property rights but also reduces the tax burden. Astute corporate executives therefore can lower the cost of access to capital by finding new ways of working within the framework of direct investor ownership. Lower capital costs can be achieved by leasing equipment instead of owning it, as well as buying inputs and components from employee-owned facilities. Lower capital costs in turn enhance American companies' competitiveness in the global economy.

Shared ownership of specific productive assets, moreover, predates the corporation by several hundred years. As early as the thirteenth century, one could buy shares in the royalties from a silver mine near Siena, and shares were available even earlier in salt mines, copper mines, and metal works. The regular practice of shared ownership of galleys in the Mediterranean trade dates back before the fifteenth century. "Kuxen" shares in the royalties from Central European mines were widely traded in the sixteenth century. Shared ownership of mills, dams, and drainage systems was also prevalent in Europe during the Middle Ages. Such arrangements not only provided a means of risk sharing but, for practical purposes, a full measure of limited liability. They were all-equity arrangements and the worst that could happen was for the ship to be lost or the mine play out—in which case each shareholder stood to lose the amount invested, but no more.

Thus the renewal of direct investment is not a radical step into a new order, but rather a return to long-established tradition in the conduct of commerce and industry. Dequity financing arrangements are playing a significant role in effecting that transformation.

NOTES

1. Adolph Berle and Gardner Means, *The Modern Corporation*, p. 244.
2. Quoted in *Barron's*, October 16, 1989, p. 8.
3. Boris I. Bittker and James S. Eustice, *Federal Income Taxation*, p. 36.
4. Gordon Donaldson, *Managing Corporate Wealth*, pp. 3 and 22.
5. Bradford Cornell and Alan Shapiro, "Corporate Stakeholders," pp. 5–14.
6. Fernand Braudel, *The Wheels of Commerce*, p. 235.
7. In *Keller v. CIR*, the Tax Court observed, "The [legislative] policy favoring the recognition of corporations as entities independent of their shareholders requires that we not ignore the corporate form so long as the corporation actually conducts business." Source: Bittker and Eustice, p. 24.
8. *Barron's*, February 12, 1990, p. 28.

REFERENCES

Barron's, October 16, 1989, p. 8.

Barron's, February 12, 1990, p. 28.

Berle, Adolph, and Gardner Means. *The Modern Corporation and Private Property*, rev. ed. (New York: Harcourt, Brace & World, 1967, p. 244) (First ed., New York: Macmillan, 1932).

Bittker, Boris I., and James S. Eustice. *Federal Income Taxation of Corporations and Shareholders*, 5th ed. (Boston: Warren, Gorhjam & Lamont, 1987), p. 36.

Braudel, Fernand. *The Wheels of Commerce,* Vol. II, *Civilization and Capitalism* (New York: Harper & Row, 1982), p. 235.

Cornell, Bradford, and Alan Shapiro. "Corporate Stakeholders and Corporate Finance," *Financial Management* 16 (Spring 1987), pp. 5–14.

Donaldson, Gordon. *Managing Corporate Wealth* (New York: Praeger, 1984), pp. 3 and 22.

Name Index

Subject Index

About the Authors

ANDREW H. CHEN is Distinguished Professor of Finance at the Edwin L. Cox School of Business, Southern Methodist University. He has authored or co-authored more than 50 articles for academic and professional publications, and is currently an editor of *Research in Finance*.

JOHN W. KENSINGER is Associate Professor of Finance at North Texas University (Denton). His articles and research papers have appeared in the *Journal of Financial Economics*, *Research in Finance*, *Managerial and Decision Economics*, and the *Journal of Applied Corporate Finance*, among other publications.